# BELGIUM TRAVEL GUIDE

Captivating
Adventures through
Must-See Places,

Local Culture, Belgian Landmarks,
Hidden Gems, and More

© **Copyright 2025- All rights reserved.**

The content contained within this book may not be reproduced, duplicated, or transmitted without direct written permission from the author or the publisher.

Under no circumstances will any blame or legal responsibility be held against the publisher, or author, for any damages, reparation, or monetary loss due to the information contained within this book, either directly or indirectly.

**Legal Notice:**

This book is copyright protected. It is only for personal use. You cannot amend, distribute, sell, use, quote, or paraphrase any part, or the content within this book, without the consent of the author or publisher.

**Disclaimer Notice:**

Please note the information contained within this document is for educational and entertainment purposes only. All effort has been executed to present accurate, up-to-date, reliable, and complete information. No warranties of any kind are declared or implied. Readers acknowledge that the author is not engaging in the rendering of legal, financial, medical, or professional advice. The content within this book has been derived from various sources. Please consult a licensed professional before attempting any techniques outlined in this book.

By reading this document, the reader agrees that under no circumstances is the author responsible for any losses, direct or indirect, that are incurred as a result of the use of the information contained within this document, including, but not limited to, errors, omissions, or inaccuracies.

***Disclaimer: At the time of going to print, all information in this guide was accurate; however, travelers are encouraged to verify details, prices, and schedules as they may change over time.***

# Welcome Aboard, Discover
# Your Limited-Time Free Bonus!

Hello, traveler! Welcome to the Captivating Travels family, and thanks for grabbing a copy of this book! Since you've chosen to join us on this journey we'd like to offer you something special.

Check out the link below for a FREE Ultimate Travel Checklist eBook & Printable PDF to make your travel planning stress-free and enjoyable.

But that's not all - you'll also gain access to our exclusive email list with even more free e-books and insider travel tips. Well, what are you waiting for? Click the link below to join and embark on your next adventure with ease.

**Access your bonus here: https://livetolearn.lpages.co/checklist/**
**Or, Scan the QR code!**

# TABLE OF CONTENTS

| | |
|---|---|
| **Introduction:** Welcome to Belgium! | 6 |
| **Chapter 1:** Getting to and Around Belgium | 14 |
| **Chapter 2:** Iconic Landmarks & Must-See Sights | 23 |
| **Chapter 3:** Belgium's Most Beautiful Natural Wonders | 37 |
| **Chapter 4:** Exploring Brussels – Belgium's Capital | 46 |
| **Chapter 5:** Bruges – A Fairy-tale City | 57 |
| **Chapter 6:** Ghent – A Medieval Treasure | 69 |
| **Chapter 7:** Antwerp – The Diamond City | 81 |
| **Chapter 8:** Hidden Gems & Off-the-Beaten-Path Destinations | 94 |
| **Chapter 9:** Belgium's Food Scene – A Culinary Journey | 108 |
| **Chapter 10:** Belgium for Adventure Seekers | 119 |
| **Chapter 11:** Day Trips & Excursions Beyond the Cities | 128 |
| **Chapter 12:** Where to Stay – Best Areas & Accommodations | 137 |
| **Chapter 13:** Belgium's Culture, Customs & Etiquette | 144 |
| **Chapter 14:** Understanding Belgium's Currency & Money Matters | 151 |
| **Chapter 15:** Seasonal Events & Festivities | 156 |
| **Chapter 16:** Shopping & Souvenirs | 163 |
| **Chapter 17:** Most Recommended Spots by Travelers | 171 |

**Chapter 18:** The 20 Best Photo Spots in Belgium . . . . . . . . . . . . . . 176

**Chapter 19:** Belgium Itineraries – Explore at Your
              Own Pace . . . . . . . . . . . . . . . . . . . . . . . . . . . . . . . . . . . . . 182

**Appendix:** Where to Find Key Landmarks in This Guide . . . . . . 190

Here's another book by Captivating Travels
that you might like. . . . . . . . . . . . . . . . . . . . . . . . . . . . . . . . . . . . . . . . 196

Welcome Aboard, Discover Your Limited-Time
Free Bonus! . . . . . . . . . . . . . . . . . . . . . . . . . . . . . . . . . . . . . . . . . . . . . . . 197

Image Sources . . . . . . . . . . . . . . . . . . . . . . . . . . . . . . . . . . . . . . . . . . . 198

# INTRODUCTION: WELCOME TO BELGIUM!

*Bienvenue! Welkom!*

> Welcome to Belgium, a small but mighty country at the heart of Western Europe. Known for its storybook towns, medieval castles, world-class chocolates, and legendary beers, Belgium is a dream destination for travelers who love history, culture, and food.

Whether you're strolling through the stunning Grand Place in Brussels, taking a boat ride through the canals of Bruges, or tasting the world's best fries, waffles, and Trappist beers, Belgium is filled with unforgettable experiences waiting for you.

In this guide, we'll help you explore Belgium's top landmarks, hidden gems, and cultural traditions, giving you everything you need for an amazing adventure.

**A snapshot of Ghent, Belgium**

Map of Belgium

## QUICK FACTS & HISTORY

**Location:** Western Europe, bordered by France, Germany, the Netherlands, and Luxembourg

**Capital City:** Brussels

**Languages:** Dutch, French, and German (depending on the region)
**Currency:** Euro (€)

**Time Zone:** Central European Time (CET)

Belgium has a rich and complex history that dates back centuries. Once part of the Roman Empire, it later became a center of trade and power in medieval Europe. Today, Belgium is home to key European Union institutions, making it a key player in international politics.

**A beautiful sunset setting in Belgium**

Belgium is divided into three main regions:

- ✦ **Flanders (Dutch-speaking north)** – Home to cities such as Bruges, Ghent, and Antwerp, known for stunning architecture and art.
- ✦ **Wallonia (French-speaking south)** – A region of rolling hills, historic towns, and beautiful castles.
- ✦ **Brussels (the bilingual capital region)** – A cosmopolitan city full of museums, grand squares, and European institutions.

**Brussels**

## WHY VISIT BELGIUM?

**National Basilica of the Sacred Heart in Koekelberg, Brussels**[1]

- **Stunning Cities & Architecture** – Wander through medieval streets, grand cathedrals, and charming market squares.
- **A Food Lover's Paradise** – Enjoy Belgian waffles, chocolate, fries, and the best beers in the world.
- **Rich Culture & Art Scene** – Home to Renaissance painters, comic books, and modern design.
- **Perfect for History Buffs** – Visit World War battlefields, medieval castles, and Gothic churches.
- **Compact & Easy to Explore** – You can travel between cities in under an hour.

A traditional Belgian dish of moules-frites[2]

## BEST TIMES TO VISIT BELGIUM

No matter when you visit Belgium, each season brings its own charm, from **springtime blooms and summer festivals** to **autumn's golden landscapes and winter's festive magic**.

Here are some highlights from every season that you can expect:

- **Spring (March-May):** Best for mild weather, blooming flowers, and fewer crowds. A great time for sightseeing and outdoor activities.
- **Summer (June-August):** Peak tourist season with warm weather, lively festivals, and outdoor dining. Expect bigger crowds in cities like Bruges and Brussels.
- **Autumn (September-November):** A fantastic time to visit for fall colors, wine festivals, and comfortable temperatures. Fewer tourists make it easier to explore.
- **Winter (December-February):** Perfect for magical Christmas markets, cozy cafés, and festive decorations. A great time to enjoy Belgian hot chocolate.

Grote Markt square in Brugge

The Collegiate Church of St. Bartholomew in Liège, Belgium

## WHAT YOU CAN EXPECT IN THIS GUIDE

**Are you ready to savor delicious waffles in some of Belgium's most famous cities?**

- **Complete Travel Insights** – Get the best recommendations for Brussels, Bruges, Ghent, Antwerp, and more.
- **Hidden Gems & Local Secrets** – Discover lesser-known spots most tourists miss.
- **Food & Drink Guide** – Find the best waffles, fries, chocolate, and beer.
- **Full-Color Maps & Photos** – Navigate easily with detailed visuals.
- **QR Codes for Instant Access** – Scan QR codes to access updated travel info, interactive maps, and transit guides.
- **Accommodation & Itinerary Suggestions** – Plan your stay with 3-day, 7-day, and 10-day itineraries.
- **Practical Travel Tips** – Learn about local customs, currency, and essential phrases to make your trip smooth.

Belgium is a place where history meets modern charm, and every street tells a story. Get ready to explore its fairy-tale towns, savor delicious treats, and make unforgettable memories.

## *Your Belgian adventure starts now!*

*Map of Belgium*

# CHAPTER 1
# GETTING TO AND AROUND BELGIUM

Belgium's central location in Europe makes it one of the easiest countries to reach and explore. With its efficient transportation network, you can travel between cities in under an hour, whether by train, bus, or car. In this chapter, you'll find everything you need to know about getting to Belgium and navigating the country with ease.

**Brussels Airport[3]**

Map view of Brussels Airport⁴

## GETTING TO BELGIUM

### BY AIR: MAJOR AIRPORTS AND AIRLINES

Belgium has several airports, but the **main international gateway** is **Brussels Airport (BRU)**, located just 12 km from the city center in the Zaventem .

*Brussels Airport Information*

### Other key airports include:

+ **Brussels South Charleroi Airport (CRL)** – Popular for budget airlines like Ryanair and Wizz Air.

**Map view of Brussels South Charleroi Airport**[5]

✈ **Antwerp International Airport (ANR)** – A small airport mainly serving European destinations.

**Map view of Antwerp International Airport**[6]

✦ **Liège Airport (LGG)** - Focuses on cargo and some passenger flights.

Map view of Liège Airport[7]

From the airport, you can easily reach your destination by **train, bus, or taxi**. The train from **Brussels Airport to the city center takes just 20 minutes**.

## BY TRAIN: HIGH-SPEED RAIL CONNECTIONS

**Brussels-South railway station**

Belgium is well-connected to major European cities via high-speed trains:

+ **Eurostar** – Includes direct routes between Brussels and London in under 2 hours.
+ **ICE & TGV** – High-speed options for Germany and France.

Brussels' **main train hub, Bruxelles-Midi (Brussels-South),** is where most international trains arrive.

## BY BUS: BUDGET-FRIENDLY TRAVEL

Long-distance buses like **FlixBus** offer affordable connections between Belgium and neighboring countries. Though slower than trains, they are a good budget option.

## BY CAR: DRIVING INTO BELGIUM

If you're **road-tripping across Europe**, Belgium's highways make it easy to drive in from **France, Germany, the Netherlands, or Luxembourg**. Major roads include the **E40 (east-west) and E19 (north-south)**.

Unlike some European countries, Belgium's highways do not have tolls, except for the **Liefkenshoek Tunnel in Antwerp**.

## GETTING AROUND BELGIUM

## BY TRAIN: THE BEST WAY TO TRAVEL

Belgium's **train system is fast, efficient, and well-connected**, making it the best way to explore the country. The **SNCB (National Railway Company of Belgium)** operates frequent trains between major cities:

+ **Brussels to Bruges** – 1 hour
+ **Brussels to Antwerp** – 45 minutes
+ **Bruges to Ghent** – 25 minutes

*SNCB Information*

### Money-Saving Tip

Get a **Belgian Rail Pass** for unlimited travel on domestic routes. If you're under 26, the **Youth Ticket** offers huge discounts.

## BY BUS & TRAM: GREAT FOR LOCAL TRAVEL

An electric bus operated by STIB/MIVB[8]

While trains are best for intercity travel, buses and trams are great for **shorter distances**. Public transport is **run by different companies depending on the region**:

+ **STIB/MIVB (Brussels)** – Metro, buses, and trams in the capital.

+ **De Lijn (Flanders)** – Buses and trams in cities like Antwerp and Bruges.

+ **TEC (Wallonia)** – Bus services across the French-speaking region.

A De Lijn tram in Ghent⁹

## BY BIKE: A FUN AND SCENIC OPTION

Belgium is a **bike-friendly country**, especially in cities like **Ghent, Antwerp, and Bruges**. Many streets have **dedicated bike lanes**, and rentals are widely available. Some cities offer **bike-sharing programs** like **Blue-bike in Flanders**.

*Blue-bike information*

## BY TAXI & RIDE-SHARING APPS

Taxis in Belgium can be expensive, and they **must be booked in advance** in most cities. Instead, ride-sharing apps like **Uber and Bolt** are popular and often more affordable.

## BY CAR: DO YOU NEED ONE?

While **renting a car** is useful for exploring the **countryside or Ardennes region**, it's unnecessary in major cities due to **excellent public transport and limited parking**.

### Driving Tips:

- Belgium has **strict traffic laws**, including fines for speeding and low-emission zones in **Brussels and Antwerp**.
- Speed limits: **120 km/h (highways), 50 km/h (cities), 30 km/h (residential zones)**.

### Money-Saving Tips for Transportation

- **Book train tickets early** for discounts on high-speed routes.
- **Use travel passes** like the **Go Pass (for youth)** or **Rail Pass (adults)** for unlimited domestic train rides.
- **Bike rentals** are a cheap and scenic way to explore cities.
- **Public transport apps** like **SNCB, De Lijn, and TEC** help you check schedules and fares easily.

Belgium's compact size and efficient transport system make getting around **quick, easy, and stress-free**. Whether you choose the speed of trains, the convenience of buses, or the charm of biking, your journey through Belgium will be smooth and enjoyable.

# CHAPTER 2
# ICONIC LANDMARKS & MUST-SEE SIGHTS

Belgium is home to some of the most iconic and unique landmarks in Europe, blending medieval charm with modern flair. This chapter introduces you to the must-see sights — places that define Belgium's heritage, creativity, and national pride. Whether you're drawn to historic squares, gothic cathedrals, castles, or futuristic architecture, these landmarks are not to be missed.

A scene from Brugge, Belgium[10]

## GRAND PLACE, BRUSSELS

The **Grand Place** is Brussels' most famous attraction and a **UNESCO World Heritage Site**. This magnificent central square is surrounded by **ornately decorated guildhalls**, the **Brussels Town Hall**, and the **King's House (Maison du Roi)**, which now houses the **Brussels City Museum**.

Every building tells a story, with **gold-trimmed facades, carved statues**, and rich symbolism that reflects the city's prosperous history as a major trade center. The square is especially magical when illuminated at night or during the **Flower Carpet**, a biennial event in August where thousands of begonias form intricate, colorful patterns across the cobblestones.

The Grand Place is a lively hub for **festivals, open-air concerts, and holiday markets**, and it's just steps from iconic nearby sights like the **Galeries Royales Saint-Hubert**, a luxury glass-roofed arcade, and the ever-popular **Manneken Pis**, a small bronze statue with a big personality that is often dressed in costumes for special events and holidays.

*Grote Markt information*

**Map view of Grote Markt**[11]

# ATOMIUM, BRUSSELS

**The Atomium**[12]

Built for the **1958 World's Fair (Expo 58)**, the Atomium has become one of Belgium's most recognizable structures. Standing 102 meters tall, it represents an **iron crystal magnified 165 billion times** and consists of nine interconnected steel spheres.

Inside, visitors can explore **science and design exhibitions**, interactive displays about the building's history, and panoramic views from the top sphere. The upper sphere also houses a **restaurant** with sweeping views over Brussels.

It's an engaging stop for architecture fans, families, and anyone curious about Belgium's post-war innovation and futuristic ambition. The nearby **Mini-Europe park** is also worth a visit, featuring miniature models of iconic European monuments.

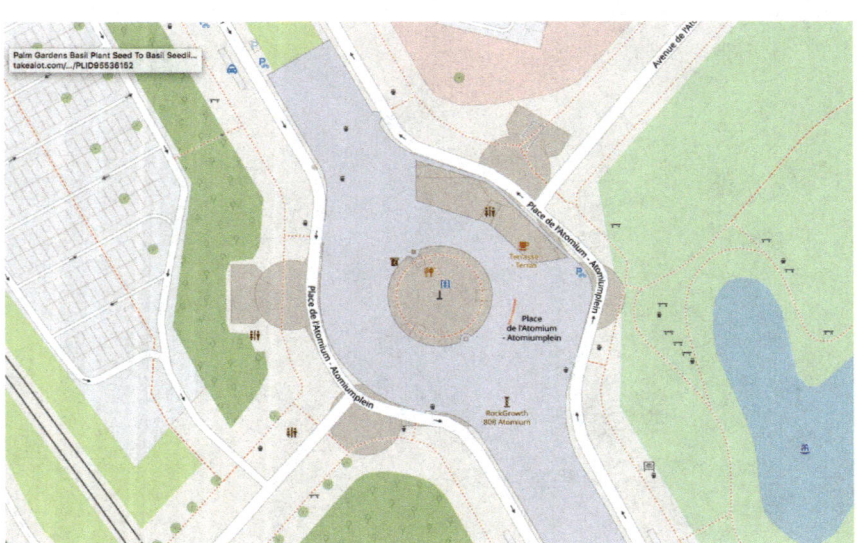

Map view of Atomium, Brussels[13]

## HISTORIC CENTER OF BRUGES

The historic center of Bruges is a perfectly preserved medieval town that looks like something out of a fairy-tale. Recognized as a **UNESCO World Heritage Site**, the city is known for its **canals, cobbled lanes, Gothic buildings, and peaceful squares**.

A must-see is the **Markt (Market Square)**, dominated by the **Belfry of Bruges**, an 83-meter-tall medieval bell tower. Climb the 366 steps for panoramic views of the city's red rooftops and winding waterways. The **Provincial Court**, horse-drawn carriages, and local markets make the square feel timeless.

**The Belfry of Bruges**

A walk through **Burg Square** reveals the **Basilica of the Holy Blood**, known for its sacred relic and unique blend of Romanesque and Gothic styles. Bruges is also famous for its **lace shops, artisan chocolatiers**, and peaceful **canal boat tours**, which provide a relaxing way to see the city's architecture from the water.

**Map view of the Markt in Bruges**[14]

# GRAVENSTEEN CASTLE, GHENT

*Gravensteen Castle in Ghent*

Right in the heart of Ghent, **Gravensteen Castle** — "Castle of the Counts" — stands as a powerful reminder of the Middle Ages. Built in 1180, it was the former residence of the Counts of Flanders and features **thick stone walls, battlements, and towers**.

Inside, visitors can explore **armories, torture chambers, a knight's hall**, and exhibits on medieval justice. A highlight is the **audio guide**, which offers a humorous yet informative journey through the castle's dark and dramatic history.

From the rooftop, you'll get stunning views over Ghent's canals, cathedrals, and city streets. It's a family-friendly, interactive experience and a top cultural attraction in East Flanders.

*Scan the QR Code for more information.*

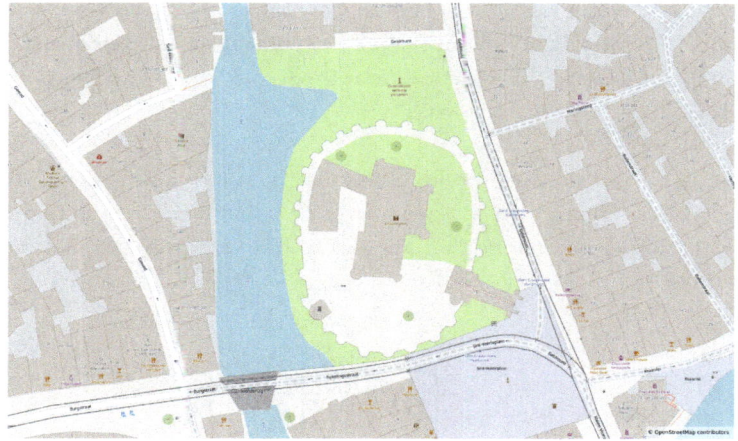

Map view of Gravensteen Castle[15]

## CATHEDRAL OF OUR LADY, ANTWERP

The **Cathedral of Our Lady** (Onze-Lieve-Vrouwekathedraal) is a Gothic masterpiece that took nearly two centuries to complete and is one of the tallest church in the Benelux region. Its **123-meter spire** dominates Antwerp's skyline and can be seen from nearly every corner of the city.

Cathedral of Our Lady, Antwerp[16]

Inside the cathedral, visitors will find an incredible collection of art, including four works by **Peter Paul Rubens**, one of Belgium's greatest Baroque painters. The highlights include **"The Elevation of the Cross"** and **"The Descent from the Cross,"** which hang in the massive nave.

The cathedral is also rich in religious artifacts, stained glass windows, and quiet chapels. Though it's a place of worship, it doubles as an art museum and architectural marvel that appeals to both spiritual travelers and art lovers alike.

*Scan the QR Code for more information.*

**Map view of the Cathedral of Our Lady**[17]

# BATTLEFIELD OF WATERLOO

The Lion's Mound at the Battlefied of Waterloo

Located just south of Brussels, the **Battlefield of Waterloo** is where **Napoleon Bonaparte was famously defeated** in 1815. This historic site includes the **Lion's Mound**, an artificial hill topped with a lion statue symbolizing the Allied victory. Climb the 226 steps to see sweeping views of the battlefield.

The newly designed **Memorial 1815 Visitor Center** offers a powerful multimedia experience with **films, exhibits, original artifacts**, and recreations of the battlefield. The nearby **Hougoumont Farm** — a key stronghold during the battle—has also been preserved and opened to visitors.

The Waterloo site is more than a battlefield; it's a **place of memory and education**, ideal for history buffs and families alike.

*Scan the QR Code for more information about the Visitor Centre.*

# THE ROYAL PALACE, BRUSSELS

The Royal Palace of Brussels

The **Royal Palace of Brussels** is the official palace of the Belgian King, used for ceremonial functions and public receptions. Located on **Place des Palais**, directly across from **Brussels Park**, it is one of the city's most elegant buildings.

During the **summer months**, the palace opens its doors to the public. Inside, you'll see a mix of **neoclassical architecture, marble staircases, chandeliers**, and beautifully decorated halls. Highlights include the **Throne Room, Mirror Room**, and exhibitions on Belgian monarchy and heritage.

Even when closed, the exterior is a lovely backdrop for photos, especially paired with a walk through the nearby **Royal Park** or the neighboring **Magritte Museum**.

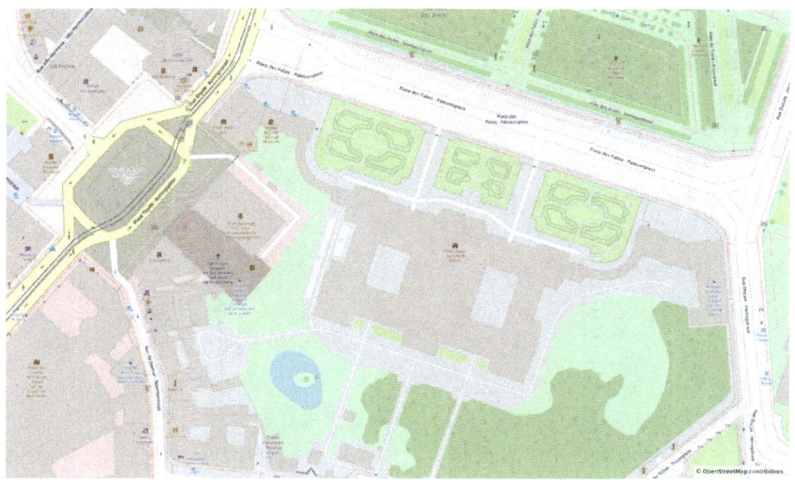

Map view of the Royal Palace of Brussels[8]

## BASILICA OF THE HOLY BLOOD, BRUGES

Tucked away in **Burg Square**, this basilica is one of Bruges' most spiritual and architecturally intriguing sites. It consists of two chapels: a **Romanesque lower chapel** and a **Gothic upper chapel**, richly decorated with gold leaf and vivid murals.

The Basilica of the Holy Blood[19]

The church is famous for housing a **relic believed to contain a cloth with the blood of Christ**, brought to Bruges during the Second Crusade. This relic is paraded through the city each year during the **Procession of the Holy Blood**, a UNESCO-recognized event.

Quiet, ornate, and full of history, the basilica offers a **peaceful moment of reflection** in the heart of the city.

## EUROPEAN QUARTER, BRUSSELS

Parc du Cinquantenaire in the European Quarter

The **European Quarter** is where politics meets architecture in Brussels. As home to the **European Parliament, the European Commission, and the Council of the EU**, this area showcases modern glass buildings, sculptures, and multilingual energy.

Visitors can tour the **Parlamentarium**, a high-tech visitors' center offering interactive exhibits on the history, function, and role of the European Union. It's a great stop for anyone curious about how international politics works.

Also nearby are peaceful green spaces like **Parc Leopold** and the impressive **Berlaymont Building**, the headquarters of the European Commission.

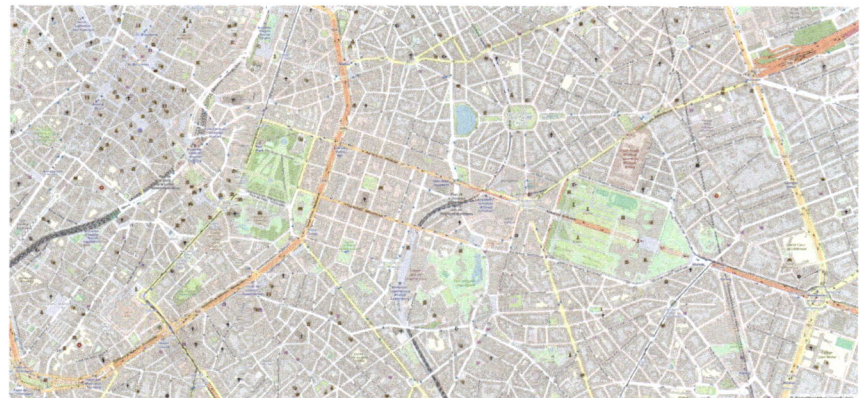

Map view of the European Quarter[20]

## THE CAVES OF HAN-SUR-LESSE

Located in the **Ardennes region**, the **Caves of Han** are one of Europe's most impressive natural underground attractions. Formed over thousands of years by the Lesse River, these limestone caves stretch for over 2 km and feature **massive chambers, dripping stalactites, and an underground river**.

The historic tram at the caves[21]

The guided tour begins with a vintage tram ride into the reserve, followed by a journey through lit chambers with natural acoustics and dramatic rock formations.

Visitors can also explore the **Han Wildlife Park**, home to European bison, lynx, brown bears, and wolves. The site offers a great combination of nature, geology, and conservation.

Belgium's landmarks are more than just sightseeing stops—they are part of the nation's **living story**, offering glimpses into its **glorious past, vibrant present, and thoughtful future**. These must-see sights give every traveler a deeper appreciation for Belgium's diversity, creativity, and timeless appeal.

# CHAPTER 3
# BELGIUM'S MOST BEAUTIFUL NATURAL WONDERS

While Belgium is often celebrated for its cities and culture, its natural beauty is just as rewarding. From rolling forests and rocky cliffs to vast coastal dunes and underground caves, Belgium offers a surprising variety of landscapes for nature lovers and adventure seekers. This chapter takes you to the most impressive natural spots in the country — perfect for hiking, exploring, or simply relaxing in the great outdoors.

A siberian chipmunk perches on tree branch in the Sonian Forest) of Brussels

# THE ARDENNES: BELGIUM'S WILD SOUTH

An aerial view of the Ardennes

The **Ardennes** is Belgium's most iconic natural region. Stretching across the southern provinces of **Luxembourg, Namur, and Liège**, it's a landscape of **dense forests, misty hills, limestone cliffs, and fast-flowing rivers**.

## THIS REGION IS PERFECT FOR *OUTDOOR ACTIVITIES* SUCH AS:

- **Hiking and cycling** through quiet trails
- **Kayaking on the Lesse or Ourthe Rivers**
- **Caving, rock climbing, and ziplining** in natural parks
- **Wildlife spotting**, including deer, wild boars, and birds of prey

Charming villages like **La Roche-en-Ardenne, Bouillon,** and **Durbuy** (known as the world's smallest city) are perfect bases for exploring the region. In autumn, the forests come alive with color, while winter turns the hills into a quiet, snowy escape.

# HOGE KEMPEN NATIONAL PARK

**Beautiful autumn weather in Hoge Kempen National Park**

Located in **Limburg province**, **Hoge Kempen** is Belgium's first and only national park. Covering more than **5,000 hectares**, the park is a peaceful retreat with **pine forests, heathlands, sand dunes, and lakes**.

With over **200 kilometers of marked trails**, it's a paradise for hikers, cyclists, and horseback riders. One of the most popular spots s the **Connecterra gateway**, where you can hike up former mining slag heaps for stunning panoramic views.

Visitors can also enjoy **birdwatching**, visit old mining villages, and stop at park gateways like **Mechelse Heide** or **Pietersheim**, which offer educational exhibits, family activities, and cafes.

# HALLERBOS: THE ENCHANTING BLUE FOREST

*Eye-catching bluebells seen at Hallerbos[22]*

Every spring, the forest of **Hallerbos**, near Halle in **Flemish Brabant**, transforms into a **sea of blooming bluebells**. From mid-April to early May, the forest floor becomes a vibrant carpet of purple-blue flowers beneath tall, slender beech trees.

Walking through the **peaceful trails** during this bloom is a magical experience—especially in the early morning when mist clings to the trees and sunlight filters through the canopy.

The forest is free to visit, with marked paths and parking nearby. It's one of Belgium's most **photographed and beloved natural scenes**, drawing visitors from across Europe during its short blooming window.

## THE MEUSE RIVER VALLEY

**An aerial view of the Meuse River**

The **Meuse River** winds through the southern part of Belgium, carving out a scenic route of **cliffs, castles, river towns, and forested hills**. Towns like **Dinant**, with its cliffside citadel and riverside promenade, are popular highlights.

The valley is a favorite for:

- **Boat rides and river cruises**
- **Hiking and cycling** along the water
- **Visiting cliff-top fortresses** like the **Citadel of Dinant or Namur**
- **Exploring caves**, such as the Grotte La Merveilleuse in Dinant.

In fall, the valley becomes especially beautiful with autumn foliage reflected in the river—perfect for a scenic road trip or weekend escape.

# THE SONIAN FOREST (FORÊT DE SOIGNES)

**A small chapel in the Sonian Forest**[23]

Just outside of Brussels lies the **Sonian Forest**, a vast green space covering over **4,000 hectares**. Once part of a royal hunting ground, this beech-dominated forest is now a UNESCO World Heritage Site and a peaceful escape for locals and visitors alike.

## VISITORS CAN ENJOY:

- **Peaceful walking and cycling trails**
- **Wildlife observation**, including foxes, deer, and owls
- **Historic abbeys and old chapels**, like **Rouge-Cloître**
- **Easy access from Brussels by tram, bus, or bike**

The forest plays an important ecological role and is a rare example of an ancient woodland that has survived so close to a capital city.

# THE NORTH SEA COAST

**The Ostend promenade**[24]

Belgium's coast may be small, but it offers **sandy beaches, coastal dunes, and laid-back seaside towns** perfect for a relaxing break. Stretching about **65 kilometers**, the coast is connected by the **Coastal Tram**, one of the longest tram lines in the world, running from **De Panne** to **Knokke-Heist**.

## TOP SPOTS INCLUDE:

+ **Ostend** – Belgium's most vibrant beach town, with museums, art galleries, and a lively boardwalk
+ **De Haan** – A quiet, picturesque resort with Belle Époque architecture
+ **Nieuwpoort and Blankenberge** – Ideal for families, kite surfing, and seafood

Summer is the most popular time to visit, but the coast is also peaceful in the shoulder seasons for long walks and fresh sea air.

Map view of Ostend[25]

## HIGH FENS (HAUTES FAGNES)

Located in the **East Cantons near the German border**, the **High Fens** is Belgium's highest and most mysterious natural area. It's a windswept plateau of **peat bogs, heathlands, and wetlands**, often shrouded in fog, with a landscape more like Scotland than central Europe.

The boardwalk seen at sunset[26]

## POPULAR ACTIVITIES INCLUDE:

- **Boardwalk hiking trails**, like those near **Signal de Botrange**, Belgium's highest point
- **Cross-country skiing** in winter
- **Birdwatching and photography**, especially in early morning light

The **Eifel-Ardennes Nature Park** and nearby towns like **Eupen** and **Malmedy** make great starting points for exploring this unique environment.

*Scan the QR Code to read more about the park.*

From wild forests to windswept coastlines, Belgium's natural wonders offer **space to breathe, adventure to discover, and beauty in every season**. These landscapes show a different side of the country — one filled with **quiet trails, peaceful waters, and ancient woodlands**. Whether you're an active explorer or a nature lover seeking stillness, Belgium's outdoors is waiting to be discovered.

CHAPTER

# 4 EXPLORING BRUSSELS – BELGIUM'S CAPITAL

**Brussels is more than just Belgium's capital. It's also the de facto hub of the European Union, a center for politics, art, gastronomy, and history. Known for its stunning architecture, museums, street art, and food, Brussels is a dynamic mix of old-world charm and modern energy. In this chapter, you'll explore the city's best sights, neighborhoods, cultural experiences, and insider tips for making the most of your visit.**

Brussels[27]

*Interactive map of Brussels*

## GETTING TO KNOW BRUSSELS

Brussels offers several incredible landmarks for visitors to discover[28]

Brussels is a **bilingual city** (French and Dutch), although English is widely spoken in tourist areas. It's divided into distinct neighborhoods, each offering its own personality and attractions. The city center is compact and walkable, and public transportation (metro, buses, trams) makes it easy to explore farther afield.

## TOP ATTRACTIONS IN BRUSSELS

### GRAND PLACE (GROTE MARKT)

The historic heart of the city, the **Grand Place** is a UNESCO World Heritage Site and a breathtaking square lined with **gilded guildhalls, the Gothic-style Town Hall**, and the **Maison du Roi**. This is where visitors come to admire architecture, take photos, and experience Brussels at its most iconic. It's especially beautiful at night when the buildings are illuminated.

BELGIUM TRAVEL GUIDE | 47

**The famous Atomium**[29]

## MANNEKEN PIS, JEANNEKE PIS & ZINNEKE PIS

These whimsical statues of a **peeing boy, girl, and dog** are beloved by locals and a fun part of Brussels' quirky character. Manneken Pis is the most famous and is often dressed in seasonal costumes. Each statue is hidden in its own corner of the city center and adds a light-hearted touch to sightseeing.

## ATOMIUM

Built for Expo 58, this futuristic steel structure in the shape of an iron atom has become a symbol of modern Brussels. Inside, visitors can tour **exhibits on design and science**, ride an elevator to a viewing platform, and dine in the panoramic **Atomium Restaurant**.

## ROYAL PALACE OF BRUSSELS

Open to the public during the summer months, the **Royal Palace** is the ceremonial residence of Belgium's royal family. Inside, explore grand halls, throne rooms, art displays, and exhibitions. The palace is located across from Brussels Park, a peaceful place to relax.

## MONT DES ARTS

One of the most scenic viewpoints in Brussels, **Mont des Arts** offers sweeping views of the city's rooftops and landmarks. The area includes beautifully landscaped gardens, fountains, and cultural institutions such as the **Magritte Museum**, **Royal Museums of Fine Arts**, and the **Musical Instruments Museum**.

## EUROPEAN QUARTER

Home to the **European Parliament, the European Commission**, and numerous embassies, the European Quarter is sleek and modern. Stop by the **Parlamentarium**, an interactive museum that explains the inner workings of the EU. It's informative and free to visit.

Mont des Arts in Brussels[30]

# BEST NEIGHBORHOODS TO EXPLORE

## SABLON (LE SABLON)

Church of Our Blessed Lady of the Sablon[31]

A sophisticated district filled with **antique shops, art galleries, chocolate boutiques**, and weekend markets. Don't miss the **Church of Our Blessed Lady of the Sablon**, a stunning Gothic church that once served the city's nobility.

*More information about the Church of Our Blessed Lady of the Sablon*

## MAROLLES (LES MAROLLES)

*A panoramic view of the famous flea market*[32]

A lively, bohemian neighborhood known for its **flea market at Place du Jeu de Balle**, vintage stores, and artistic murals. It's a great area to discover local life and dig through treasures at antique shops

## IXELLES & SAINT-GILLES

Trendy and multicultural, these residential areas offer **vibrant nightlife, global cuisine**, and **Art Nouveau architecture**. They're popular with locals and are home to famous buildings designed by Victor Horta, a pioneer of Art Nouveau.

*Interactive map of Saint-Gilles*

# FOOD AND DRINK IN BRUSSELS

**Traditional Belgian waffles**[33]

Brussels is a **foodie's paradise**. From fine dining to street snacks, there's something for every palate. Be sure to try:

- **Belgian Waffles** – Available in soft Brussels style or sweet Liège style
- **Fries (Frites)** – Served in cones with a wide range of sauces
- **Moules-frites** – Mussels cooked in white wine or cream, served with fries
- **Belgian Chocolate** – Visit artisan chocolatiers like Pierre Marcolini, Neuhaus, or Leonidas
- **Beer** – Enjoy a glass at a local beer café such as Delirium, with its world-record beer selection

For traditional Belgian fare, look for **stoofvlees** (beef stew), **waterzooi** (creamy chicken or fish stew), and **carbonnade flamande** (Flemish beef braised in beer).

*Interactive map of chocolatiers in Brussels*

*More information about Delirium*

## SHOPPING IN BRUSSELS

Galeries Royales Saint-Hubert[34]

Head to the **Galeries Royales Saint-Hubert**, a grand covered arcade filled with luxury boutiques, cafes, and chocolate shops. For local finds, browse markets like **Place du Jeu de Balle Flea Market** or visit **Rue Antoine Dansaert** for Belgian fashion designers.

# MUSEUMS YOU SHOULDN'T MISS

**The entrance of the Royal Museums of Fine Arts**[35]

✦ **Royal Museums of Fine Arts** – Classic and modern masterpieces by Flemish and European artists

✦ **Magritte Museum** – A deep dive into surrealist René Magritte's life and work

✦ **Autoworld** – A vintage car museum perfect for automobile enthusiasts

✦ **BELvue Museum** – Tells the story of Belgium's monarchy and political history

✦ **Train World** – A fascinating railway museum housed in a historic train station

The interior of Autoworld[36]

A featured display seen at Train World[37]

## BRUSSELS TRAVEL TIPS

- ✦ **City Passes** like the **Brussels Card** give you access to museums and public transport
- ✦ Most major attractions are **closed on Mondays**—plan accordingly
- ✦ Public transport is managed by **STIB/MIVB**, with easy-to-use metro, tram, and bus lines
- ✦ Many attractions offer **free entry on the first Wednesday or Sunday of the month**

## WHY YOU'LL LOVE BRUSSELS

Brussels is a city of **contrast and creativity**—where **medieval squares meet modern skyscrapers**, and **political power meets street art**. Whether you're admiring a Gothic spire, sipping hot chocolate in a cozy café, or getting lost in a comic book mural trail, Brussels has a way of **surprising and charming every traveler**.

Spend at least **two to three days** in the city to explore its neighborhoods, museums, and markets. Brussels is more than a capital — it's **the beating heart of Belgium**.

CHAPTER

# 5 Bruges – A Fairy-Tale City

> Bruges (Brugge in Dutch) feels like stepping into a storybook. With its medieval architecture, peaceful canals, cobblestone streets, and horse-drawn carriages, it's often called one of the most beautiful cities in Europe. A UNESCO World Heritage Site, Bruges combines history, art, and romance into a small, walkable package.

In this chapter, we'll explore the must-see sights, best local experiences, and practical tips for getting the most out of your visit to this **fairy-tale Belgian city**.

A canal view of Bruges with the famous Belfry in the background[38]

## WHY VISIT BRUGES?

Bruges offers a rare combination of **preserved medieval charm** and modern comfort. It's ideal for travelers who enjoy **history, architecture, and a slower pace of travel**. Whether you're riding a canal boat, wandering quiet alleys, or tasting fresh Belgian chocolate, Bruges has a way of making you feel like you've traveled back in time.

## TOP SIGHTS IN BRUGES

### MARKT (MARKET SQUARE)

The statue of local heroes Jan Breydel and Pieter de Coninck[39]

The lively heart of Bruges, Markt is surrounded by colorful **step-gabled houses**, bustling cafes, and key landmarks. Street performers and markets often fill the square, making it perfect for people-watching.

At the center is the **statue of Jan Breydel and Pieter de Coninck**, local heroes from the 14th century who led a resistance against French rule.

## BELFRY OF BRUGES (BELFORT)

**A view of the Markt and Belfry in Bruges**[40]

Towering 83 meters above Markt Square, this medieval bell tower is one of Bruges' most famous landmarks. Visitors can **climb 366 steps** to reach the top and enjoy sweeping views of the city's rooftops and canals.

Inside, the tower houses a **carillon of 47 bells**, and you may hear live performances while exploring. Scan the below QR Code for more details:

## BURG SQUARE

**An aerial view of Burg Square**[41]

Just a short walk from the Markt, Burg Square is home to stunning architecture like the **Bruges City Hall (Stadhuis)** — one of the oldest in the Low Countries — and the **Basilica of the Holy Blood**, which houses a relic said to contain the blood of Christ.

The basilica features **two contrasting chapels**: a Romanesque lower level and a Gothic upper level adorned with stained glass and gold leaf.

## CANAL CRUISES

One of the best ways to see Bruges is from the water. Canal boat tours offer a **relaxing 30-minute journey** past quiet courtyards, historic bridges, and hidden gardens.

Guides provide **live commentary** in multiple languages, offering insights into Bruges' history and local life.

## THE BEGUINAGE (BEGIJNHOF)

**A daytime view of the Beguinage**[42]

This peaceful whitewashed complex was once home to a community of lay religious women known as beguines. Today, it remains a quiet retreat run by Benedictine nuns.

Surrounded by gardens and trees, the Beguinage is a great spot to experience the **contemplative side of medieval Bruges**.

## CHURCH OF OUR LADY (ONZE-LIEVE-VROUWEKERK)

The Church of Our Lady[43]

This Gothic church is one of the tallest brick buildings in the world and houses an extraordinary piece of art: **Michelangelo's Madonna and Child**—the first of his sculptures to leave Italy during his lifetime.

The church also contains the **tombs of Charles the Bold and Mary of Burgundy**, richly decorated in stone and metal. Scan the below QR Code for more information:

## ROZENHOEDKAAI (QUAY OF THE ROSARY)

Rozenhoedkaai (Quay of the Rosary)

This picturesque canal bend is the **most photographed spot in Bruges**. The water, gabled buildings, and weeping willows create a postcard-perfect view—especially at sunset.

Nearby, you'll find cozy cafes, art shops, and small footbridges that add to the charm.

## MUSEUMS AND CULTURE

### GROENINGEMUSEUM

This art museum houses masterpieces by **Flemish Primitives**, including works by **Jan van Eyck, Hans Memling, and Gerard David**. It's a must for art lovers who want to explore the roots of European painting.

**The Groeningemuseum**[44]

## HISTORIUM BRUGGE

Located in Markt Square, this interactive museum brings the **Golden Age of Bruges** to life through multimedia exhibits, virtual reality, and reconstructed scenes of medieval daily life. Scan the below QR Code for more details:

## CHOCO-STORY AND FRIETMUSEUM

The Frietmuseum[45]

Learn the history of Belgium's two most iconic snacks: **chocolate and fries**. These light-hearted museums are great for families or food lovers and include samples at the end of your visit.

More information about Choco-Story

More information about the Frietmuseum.

## FOOD AND DRINK IN BRUGES

Bruges is known for its **culinary excellence**, and many restaurants offer seasonal Belgian specialties using fresh, local ingredients.

## WHAT TO TRY IN BRUGES:

+ **Flemish stew (stoofvlees)** – Beef slow-cooked in beer, often served with fries
+ **Mussels (mosselen)** – Usually steamed with herbs and white wine
+ **Handmade chocolates** – Local chocolatiers like Dumon, The Chocolate Line, and Praline-te are top picks. Scan the below QR Code for an interactive map of chocolatiers in the area:

✦ **Craft beer** – Visit **Brouwerij De Halve Maan**, a brewery with its own underground beer pipeline and rooftop bar.

Bruges also offers Michelin-starred dining and cozy taverns where you can relax by candlelight after a day of exploring.

Brouwerij De Halve Maan[46]

## SHOPPING IN BRUGES

**Map view of Zilverpand**[47]

While many shops cater to tourists, there are still authentic finds if you know where to look.

Top picks include:

- **Handmade lace** – A centuries-old tradition still alive in small workshops
- **Belgian chocolate** – Look for artisan shops rather than mass-market brands
- **Local crafts and artwork** – Available at weekend markets or independent galleries

The **Zilverpand shopping district** offers a mix of boutiques, while the **Steenstraat** is the city's main shopping street with a blend of international and Belgian brands.

**Map view of Steenstraat**[48]

## TRAVEL TIPS FOR VISITING BRUGES

- ✦ **Stay overnight if possible** – Bruges is busiest with day-trippers; staying the night gives you the magic of early mornings and peaceful evenings.
- ✦ **The city is walkable** – Everything in the historic center is within easy reach on foot.
- ✦ **Rent a bike** – For exploring parks or quieter streets beyond the center.
- ✦ **Avoid weekends for a quieter visit** – Weekdays are more peaceful, especially in spring or fall.
- ✦ **Book canal tours and Belfry visits in advance during peak season.**

## HOW LONG TO STAY IN BRUGES?

**One full day** is enough to see the highlights, but staying **two to three days** allows time to explore **hidden corners, sample more food, and enjoy the slower pace**. It also gives you time for nearby day trips to places like **Damme**, **Zeebrugge**, or **Loppem Castle**.

Bruges is a place to **wander without a plan**, admire reflections in the canals, and lose yourself in its timeless beauty. With its rich history, stunning views, and quiet charm, this fairytale city is sure to become one of the most memorable parts of your journey through Belgium.

CHAPTER

# 6 GHENT – A MEDIEVAL TREASURE

> Often overshadowed by nearby Bruges and Brussels, Ghent (Gent in Dutch) is one of Belgium's best-kept secrets. A dynamic mix of medieval architecture, cutting-edge art, and a youthful vibe, Ghent is both historic and happening. The city's cobblestone streets, scenic canals, and impressive towers reflect centuries of wealth and power — while its lively bars, museums, and festivals show off its creative spirit.

In this chapter, you'll uncover what makes Ghent a **must-visit destination**: from castles and cathedrals to street art and student culture.

Early evening scene in Ghent[49]

## WHY VISIT GHENT?

**Saint Nicholas' Church in Ghent**[50]

Ghent is a city of contrasts. It has the **largest car-free city center in Belgium**, filled with **Gothic buildings**, cozy cafes, and vibrant street scenes. It's compact enough to explore on foot, yet packed with culture. Whether you're into **history, architecture, food, or music**, Ghent offers the perfect mix of old and new — with far fewer crowds than other tourist hotspots.

## TOP SIGHTS IN GHENT

### GRAVENSTEEN CASTLE

**Gravensteen Castle**[51]

Rising above the Leie River, **Gravensteen is a 12th-century fortress** right in the city center. Once home to the Counts of Flanders, it has served as a courtroom, prison, and mint. Today, it's a fully restored castle where you can tour **stone towers, dungeons, medieval weapons**, and enjoy **panoramic views** from the ramparts.

The self-guided **audio tour**, narrated with dry humor, brings the castle's history to life in an engaging way — making it fun for both adults and kids.

## ST. BAVO'S CATHEDRAL AND THE GHENT ALTARPIECE

**The interior of the cathedral**[52]

This majestic cathedral is one of Belgium's greatest treasures. Its highlight is the **Ghent Altarpiece**, also known as *The Adoration of the Mystic Lamb*, a 15th-century masterpiece by the Van Eyck brothers. Considered one of the most influential paintings in Western art, it features extraordinary detail, symbolism, and beauty.

The cathedral also houses **stunning stained glass, a baroque pulpit**, and works by Peter Paul Rubens. Be sure to see the **original restored panels**, now displayed in a high-tech viewing space.

Map view of St. Bavo's Cathedral[53]

## THE THREE TOWERS OF GHENT

Ghent's skyline is defined by **three medieval towers** lined up in a row:

+ **St. Nicholas' Church** – A 13th-century example of Scheldt Gothic architecture
+ **The Belfry of Ghent** – A UNESCO World Heritage Site and symbol of civic freedom; climb to the top for a striking city view
+ **St. Bavo's Cathedral** – Already noted above, it completes this architectural trio

These towers are best appreciated from **St. Michael's Bridge**, one of the most photogenic spots in the city.

St. Michael's Bridge, with a scenic view of the three towers

## PATERSHOL DISTRICT

This historic quarter is a maze of **narrow alleys and cobblestone streets**, once home to craftsmen and now filled with charming **restaurants, artisan shops, and cafes**. Patershol retains a village-like feel in the heart of the city, making it the perfect area to stroll in the late afternoon or enjoy a candlelit dinner.

*Scan the QR Code for a map showing Patershol District's location.*

## KORENMARKT AND GRASLEI/ KORENLEI

The **Korenmarkt** is Ghent's central square, surrounded by shops, cafes, and historical buildings. Just steps away are the **Graslei and Korenlei**, twin quays along the Leie River, lined with elegant medieval guild houses.

Grab a seat by the water, take a guided **canal boat tour**, or simply watch the city go by—this is Ghent at its most scenic and relaxed.

**An evening view of Korenlei and Graslei[54]**

Map view of Korenmarkt[55]

## MUSEUMS AND CULTURE IN GHENT

### STAM (STADSMUSEUM GENT) – GHENT CITY MUSEUM

Located in a former abbey, this modern museum walks you through **the history and future of Ghent** with interactive exhibits, models, and digital

Inside the STAM Museum[56]

installations. A great introduction to the city for first-time visitors – scan the below QR Code for more information:

## MUSEUM OF FINE ARTS (MSK)

**The Museum of Fine Arts**[57]

Houses an excellent collection of **Flemish masters**, including works by Hieronymus Bosch, Rubens, and Magritte. The galleries are quiet, well-lit, and ideal for art lovers who want a deeper cultural experience.

## S.M.A.K. (STEDELIJK MUSEUM VOOR ACTUELE KUNST) – CONTEMPORARY ART MUSEUM

**S.M.A.K**[58]

Right across from MSK, S.M.A.K. presents **experimental and provocative modern art**. Expect bold installations, multimedia exhibits, and rotating international shows.

## STREET ART AND MODERN VIBES

Ghent has a thriving **urban art scene**, thanks in part to its student population and progressive culture. Walk along **Werregarenstraatje (Graffiti Alley)** for a look at constantly changing murals and bold street art.

**Artists in Werregarenstraatje**[59]

Outside the center, you'll find **large-scale public artworks** by Belgian and international artists — part of Ghent's identity as an open-minded, forward-thinking city.

## FOOD AND DRINK IN GHENT

Ghent is known for its **creative food scene**, mixing traditional Flemish flavors with international trends and plant-based cuisine. It was one of the first cities in the world to promote **"Veggie Thursdays"**, and vegetarian options are widely available.

### WHAT TO TRY IN GHENT:

+ **Waterzooi** – A creamy stew made with chicken or fish, vegetables, and herbs
+ **Stoverij** – Flemish beef stew cooked in dark beer
+ **Cuberdons** – Local cone-shaped raspberry candy, also called "noses"
+ **Tierenteyn mustard** – Spicy mustard made locally since the 18th century

For drinks, enjoy a beer at **Dulle Griet**, a lively pub with over 500 varieties and a quirky tradition: if you order their strongest beer, you must **hand over a shoe as a deposit**.

*More information about Dulle Griet*

## SHOPPING AND MARKETS

Ghent is full of **independent shops, boutiques, and weekend markets**. Head to **Vrijdagmarkt** for clothing, crafts, and food stalls. For fresh produce and flowers, visit the **Sunday market at Bij Sint-Jacobs**.

The statue of Jacob of Artevelde seen at the Vrijdagmarkt in Ghent[60]

## TRAVEL TIPS FOR GHENT

- **Ghent is less crowded than Bruges**, especially during peak season. It's a great alternative for travelers looking to explore authentic Belgian life.
- The city is **bike-friendly** with plenty of rental options and bike lanes.
- Consider a **CityCard Gent**, which includes public transport and free entry to top attractions.
- **Public trams and buses** are run by De Lijn and are easy to navigate with mobile apps or ticket machines.
- Many museums and shops **close on Mondays**, so plan accordingly.

## HOW LONG TO STAY IN GHENT?

You can see the major sights in **one full day**, but a **two-day stay** lets you experience Ghent's **evening ambiance, local dining scene**, and lesser-known neighborhoods. The city's central location also makes it a perfect **base for day trips** to Bruges, Antwerp, or the Flemish countryside.

Ghent is a city that rewards both the casual explorer and the curious traveler. It has all the beauty of medieval Belgium with none of the crowds—plus a dash of artistic energy and youthful charm. Whether you're visiting for its cathedrals, canals, or cafés, Ghent promises an experience that's **rich, relaxed, and uniquely Belgian**.

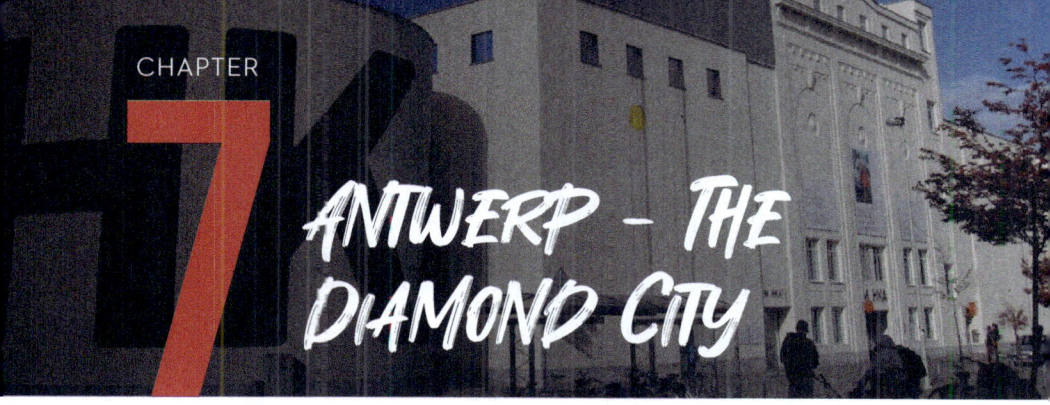

# CHAPTER 7
# ANTWERP – THE DIAMOND CITY

Antwerp (Antwerpen in Dutch) is Belgium's second-largest city and one of its most exciting. A major port, fashion capital, and global center for diamonds, Antwerp is known for its bold style, artistic heritage, and cutting-edge energy. From Gothic cathedrals and Baroque masterpieces to modern fashion boutiques and buzzing nightlife, Antwerp offers a fascinating mix of old and new.

This chapter will guide you through the city's most important landmarks, neighborhoods, shopping areas, and cultural experiences—everything you need to fall in love with **Belgium's most trendsetting city**.

Beautiful architecture in Antwerp[61]

## WHY VISIT ANTWERP?

The central station platform at Antwerp[62]

Antwerp is for travelers who enjoy **art, architecture, shopping, and vibrant street life**. It's a **creative hub** with world-class museums, thriving cafe culture, and a youthful spirit. Despite being a large city, it's easy to explore on foot or by bike, and it offers something for every kind of visitor — whether you're here for diamonds, design, or a slice of history.

## TOP ATTRACTIONS IN ANTWERP

### CATHEDRAL OF OUR LADY (ONZE-LIEVE-VROUWEKATHEDRAAL)

This **Gothic masterpiece** took 169 years to build and remains the **tallest gothic church in the Low Countries**, with its striking 123-meter spire visible across the city.

Inside, it houses some of the **greatest works of Baroque painter Peter Paul Rubens**, including *The Descent from the Cross* and *The Elevation of the Cross*. The cathedral also features **stained glass windows, soaring vaults**, and quiet chapels that reflect Antwerp's religious and artistic wealth.

**The main nave of the cathedral**[63]

## GROTE MARKT (MAIN SQUARE)

Antwerp's central square is surrounded by **Renaissance guildhalls, the Stadhuis (City Hall)**, and lively cafés. At its center is **Brabo's Monument**, a fountain depicting the legendary Roman soldier **Silvius Brabo** defeating a giant by cutting off his hand and throwing it into the river.

This myth explains the origin of Antwerp's name (*hand werpen*, or "hand throwing") and is a proud symbol of the city's independence and spirit.

## ANTWERP ZOO & CENTRAL STATION

**The entrance of Antwerp Zoo**[64]

Next to one another, these two landmarks form a stunning introduction to the city.

+ **Antwerp Central Station** is considered one of the **most beautiful train stations in the world,** with its mix of stone, iron, and glass architecture. Inside, it's a grand mix of history and functionality.

✦ **Antwerp Zoo**, one of the oldest in Europe, is home to more than 7,000 animals and offers peaceful gardens in the middle of the city. Scan the below QR Code for more information:

Inside the historic train station[65]

# MUSEUM AAN DE STROOM (MAS)

**MAS**[66]

Located in the **Eilandje district**, MAS is a modern architectural marvel covered in red sandstone and curved glass. Its exhibitions tell the story of **Antwerp's global connections**, from maritime trade to food, fashion, and world cultures.

Don't miss the **rooftop terrace**, free to access, which offers 360-degree views of the city, river, and harbor.

## RED STAR LINE MUSEUM

Housed in the old shipping warehouses of the Red Star Line, this museum shares the **stories of the two million European emigrants** who left Antwerp for America between 1873 and 1934.

With personal stories, photos, and interactive exhibits, it offers a **moving, human-centered look at migration**, identity, and hope.

## RUBENSHUIS (RUBENS HOUSE)

Once the home and studio of **Peter Paul Rubens**, this 17th-century mansion has been turned into a museum filled with the artist's work and possessions.

The courtyard of Rubenshuis[67]

The house includes **furnished rooms, a beautiful courtyard garden, and an intimate view of Rubens' life and legacy.**

## FASHION & SHOPPING IN ANTWERP

Antwerp is one of Europe's **top fashion capitals**, made famous by the **"Antwerp Six"**—a group of avant-garde designers who graduated from the Royal Academy of Fine Arts in the 1980s.

### Where to Shop:

- **Nationalestraat** – High-end boutiques and flagship stores from Belgian designers
- **Kammenstraat** – Youthful fashion, streetwear, and vintage shops
- **Meir** – Antwerp's main shopping street, with international brands and grand architecture
- **Stadsfeestzaal** – A beautifully restored shopping hall with luxury brands and cafés

If you're into fashion, don't miss the **MoMu (ModeMuseum)**, Antwerp's fashion museum showcasing design exhibitions and Belgian style through the decades. Scan the below QR Code for more information:

## DIAMONDS AND DESIGN

Diamond shops seen in the Diamond District[68]

Antwerp has been a **global diamond hub for over 500 years**. The **Diamond District**, near Central Station, is home to hundreds of traders and workshops. While many are closed to the public, some shops offer tours or certified diamond sales with expert guidance.

Design lovers should also visit **Het Zuid**, a chic neighborhood filled with **art galleries, design studios, and sleek coffee bars** — perfect for wandering on a sunny afternoon.

## MUSEUMS AND CULTURE

**Plantin Moretus Museum**

✦ **Plantin-Moretus Museum** – A UNESCO-listed site and former printing house, offering insight into the history of books, printing, and early publishing

✦ **Museum of Contemporary Art Antwerp (M HKA)** – Showcases modern Belgian and international artists

- **Royal Museum of Fine Arts (KMSKA)** – Recently renovated, this museum houses works by Rubens, Van Dyck, Ensor, and Magritte in a stunning new space

The Museum of Contemporary Art Antwerp[69]

## FOOD AND DRINK IN ANTWERP

Antwerp's cuisine is creative and global, blending Belgian classics with multicultural flavors from its large **Jewish, Moroccan, Turkish, and Congolese communities**.

### WHAT TO TRY IN ANTWERP:

- **Antwerpse Handjes** – Hand-shaped butter cookies, symbolic of the Brabo legend
- **Bolleke** – A locally brewed amber beer from De Koninck Brewery

- ✦ **Fresh seafood** – Best enjoyed near the harbor or along the Scheldt River
- ✦ **Belgian fries and waffles** – Found everywhere, but even better in small, family-run spots

For local brews and bites, visit **De Koninck Brewery**, where you can take a self-guided tour through interactive beer exhibits, then enjoy tastings in the on-site taproom. Scan the QR Code below for more information:

## NIGHTLIFE AND ENTERTAINMENT

Antwerp is lively after dark, with something for every taste:

- ✦ **Jazz cafés and rooftop bars** in Het Zuid
- ✦ **Trendy cocktail bars** in Eilandje
- ✦ **Live music venues and clubs** near Sint-Andries and the station area
- ✦ **Classical concerts and opera** at **DeSingel** and **Antwerp Opera House**

Thanks to its large student population and international community, the city feels young and energetic well into the evening.

*More information about DeSingel*

*More information about Antwerp Opera House*

## TRAVEL TIPS FOR VISITING ANTWERP

- **Antwerp is bike-friendly**, with easy-to-use rental services like Velo
- **Trams and buses**, run by De Lijn, connect the city efficiently
- Most museums and stores **are closed on Mondays**
- **Weekends bring large crowds**, especially in shopping areas—go early for quieter experiences
- **The Antwerp City Card** includes public transport, museum entry, and discounts at local restaurants

## HOW LONG TO STAY IN ANTWERP?

You can see the highlights in **a day**, but a **two- or three-day stay** allows time for deeper exploration, shopping, and relaxing in trendy neighborhoods. Antwerp also makes a great base for day trips to **Mechelen, Ghent**, or even **Rotterdam** in the Netherlands.

Antwerp is a city that thrives on **style, creativity, and energy**. Whether you come for the art, the fashion, the diamonds, or the views, this vibrant port city offers a truly **modern Belgian experience wrapped in historic beauty**.

# CHAPTER 8
# HIDDEN GEMS & OFF-THE-BEATEN-PATH DESTINATIONS

> Belgium is full of surprises beyond its major cities. In between the tourist hotspots lie charming villages, scenic river towns, ancient abbeys, and peaceful countryside that offer a slower, more personal side of the country. These hidden gems may not get as much attention as Brussels or Bruges, but they deliver authentic experiences, fewer crowds, and unforgettable scenery.

In this chapter, you'll uncover Belgium's **off-the-beaten-path destinations**—ideal for day trips, weekend escapes, or stops along a road trip.

## 1. DINANT – CLIFFTOP CASTLES AND RIVER VIEWS

Nestled in the **Meuse River Valley**, **Dinant** is one of Belgium's most photogenic small towns. Framed by **steep cliffs and the sparkling river**, its dramatic setting is matched by equally unique sights.

### HIGHLIGHTS INCLUDE:

- **Collegiate Church of Notre-Dame** – A Gothic church with a distinctive pear-shaped bell tower
- **Citadel of Dinant** – Perched high above the town, offering sweeping views and historic military exhibits
- **Grotte La Merveilleuse in Dinant** – A spectacular limestone cave system with dramatic formations and underground galleries.

**Dinant**[70]

Dinant is also the birthplace of **Adolphe Sax**, inventor of the saxophone. A riverside saxophone sculpture trail and small museum celebrate his life and music. Scan the below QR Code for more information about the museum:

**A riverside saxophone installation honoring Adolphe Sax**[71]

## 2. DURBUY - THE WORLD'S SMALLEST CITY

Topiary Park[72]

Tucked into the forested hills of the Ardennes, **Durbuy** calls itself the **smallest city in the world**, and it certainly feels like a miniature storybook town. With its **cobblestone lanes, stone houses, boutique shops**, and surrounding nature, Durbuy is the perfect quiet escape.

### THINGS TO DO:

- Stroll through the **medieval Old Town** and enjoy local cafés
- Visit the **Topiary Park**, with over 250 sculpted plant figures – scan the below QR Code for more details:

- Explore **kayaking and hiking trails** along the nearby Ourthe River

Though tiny, Durbuy offers plenty of charm, especially in spring and autumn when the village is at its most colorful.

# 3. LEUVEN - A LIVELY UNIVERSITY CITY

The famous Fonske statue, designed by Jef Claerhout, that is situated close to the town centre. This statue of a student pouring water into his head is a local favorite that also gets dressed up in playful outfits throughout the year.[73]

Home to one of Europe's oldest universities, **Leuven** blends **historic elegance** with a **young, energetic vibe**. Just 25 minutes from Brussels, it's often missed by travelers — but it's well worth a visit.

## DON'T MISS:

+ **Leuven Town Hall** - A late-Gothic masterpiece covered in statues
+ **Library and University Hall** - Rebuilt after WWI, now a symbol of resilience
+ **Oude Markt (Old Market Square)** - Known as the **"longest bar in the world,"** it's lined with lively terraces and cafés

Leuven is also home to **Stella Artois**, and you can visit the brewery on **Saturdays and Sundays** for a behind-the-scenes look (and a cold pint). It's a great city to explore on foot or by bike.

**The Stella Artois Brewery**[74]

# 4. TOURNAI – BELGIUM'S OLDEST CITY

**The Belfry of Tournai**[75]

Located near the French border, **Tournai** is one of Belgium's oldest towns and home to several architectural treasures. It's quieter than most cities, but full of history and character.

## KEY ATTRACTIONS:

✦ **Tournai Cathedral (Notre-Dame de Tournai)** – A UNESCO World Heritage Site with Romanesque and Gothic elements.

✦ **The Belfry of Tournai** – The oldest in Belgium; climb for panoramic views.

✦ **Fine Arts Museum (Musée des Beaux-Arts)** – Designed by Victor Horta, with works by Monet, Van Gogh, and more.

Tournai's compact center makes it ideal for a relaxed day of walking, photography, and discovering local crafts.

# 5. BOUILLON – MEDIEVAL CASTLES IN THE FOREST

*Bouillon[76]*

In the far south of the Ardennes near the French border, **Bouillon** offers **nature, history, and adventure**. The main attraction is the **Château de Bouillon**, a massive medieval fortress overlooking the Semois River.

## VISITORS CAN:

- Tour the fortified walls, tunnels, and dungeons
- Watch falconry demonstrations
- Hike into the surrounding forest, with marked trails offering incredible views of the valley

Bouillon is perfect for history lovers and hikers, and it makes a great base for exploring the **southern Ardennes**.

*More information about Château de Bouillon*

Château de Bouillon[77]

## 6. MECHELEN – A QUIET CHARMER BETWEEN BRUSSELS AND ANTWERP

Often overlooked in favor of its bigger neighbors, **Mechelen** is a delightful city full of **Renaissance charm and family-friendly attractions**. It's compact, peaceful, and perfect for a day trip.

### WHAT TO SEE:

- **St. Rumbold's Cathedral** – Climb the tower for sweeping city views.
- **Groot Begijnhof** – A peaceful historic quarter once home to beguines.
- **Technopolis & Planckendael Zoo** – Interactive science and nature attractions for kids and families.

More information about Technopolis

**St. Rumbold's Cathedral**[7E]

*More information about Planckendael Zoo*

Mechelen is also known for its **carillon music**, and you can often hear bell concerts from the cathedral tower during festivals and summer weekends.

# 7. OUDENAARDE – CYCLING, CASTLES, AND FLEMISH TAPESTRY

An eye-catching metallic sculpture in Oudenaarde[79]

In the heart of East Flanders, **Oudenaarde** is a quiet town with **beautiful architecture and a passion for cycling**. It's a key stop on the famous **Tour of Flanders** bike race and offers scenic countryside perfect for riding.

## TOP SIGHTS INCLUDE:

- **Town Hall and Belfry** – A Gothic masterpiece housing the **Museum of the Flemish Ardennes.**
- **Cycling Center (Centrum Ronde van Vlaanderen)** – A museum dedicated to Belgian cycling culture.
- **Nearby castles**, like **Laarne Castle**, offer peaceful walks and photo opportunities.

Oudenaarde is ideal for travelers looking to experience local life and scenic views away from the crowds.

## 8. MONS – EUROPEAN CAPITAL OF CULTURE (2015)

Saint Waltrude Collegiate Church and the Belfry of Mons[80]

Mons (Bergen in Dutch) is a city that blends **military history, vibrant art, and lively festivals**. Located in Wallonia, it gained international recognition as a **European Capital of Culture** and has since developed into a **modern cultural hub**.

## DON'T MISS:

+ **Mons Belfry** – The only Baroque-style belfry in Belgium and a UNESCO site.
+ **Grand Place of Mons** – Lined with cafes, fountains, and public art installations.
+ **Museum of Fine Arts (BAM)** – Hosts rotating exhibits of modern and contemporary art.

Mons is also close to the **Battle of Mons site**, the first battle involving British forces in World War I.

## 9. CHIMAY - MONKS, BEER, AND ABBEY LIFE

**Chimay**[81]

In Belgium's far south, **Chimay** is famous for its **Trappist beer and peaceful abbey**, made by Cistercian monks since the 1800s. It's a quiet countryside destination, perfect for relaxation and tasting traditional Belgian products.

### THINGS TO DO:

- Visit **Scourmont Abbey**, where Chimay beer and cheese are still produced.
- Tour the **Espace Chimay visitor center** to learn the history of Trappist brewing.
- Explore **hiking trails** and scenic woodlands surrounding the area.

This is a great stop for beer lovers, history buffs, or anyone looking for a **spiritual and rural experience**.

## TIPS FOR EXPLORING HIDDEN BELGIUM

- **Rent a car** to reach smaller towns, especially in the Ardennes and Wallonia.
- **Weekdays are quieter** in rural areas—perfect for peaceful sightseeing.
- Many small towns have **seasonal festivals**, so check local calendars in advance.
- Bring **comfortable walking shoes** — cobblestone streets and hilly paths are common.
- Look for **local markets** and **regional foods**—each area has its own flavors and specialties.

## DISCOVERING BELGIUM BEYOND THE GUIDEBOOKS

Belgium's beauty lies not just in its big cities, but in its **villages, valleys, abbeys, and riversides**. These hidden gems offer space to slow down, connect with local life, and explore parts of the country that most travelers never see.

Whether you want to walk through an ancient castle, paddle a river, or sip beer brewed by monks, these off-the-beaten-path destinations show a side of Belgium that's just as magical — and even more personal.

CHAPTER

# 9 BELGIUM'S FOOD SCENE – A CULINARY JOURNEY

Belgium is a food lover's paradise, where comfort meets craft in every bite. From crispy golden fries and rich stews to gourmet chocolate and world-famous beer, Belgian cuisine is deeply rooted in regional traditions, local ingredients, and a passion for flavor and quality. Whether you're dining in a grand brasserie or grabbing a waffle from a street cart, the food is almost always simple, satisfying, and full of character.

In this chapter, we'll take a delicious journey through **classic dishes, local specialties, sweet treats, and drinks** that define Belgium's culinary culture.

A Belgian waffle van seen in Brussels[82]

# CLASSIC BELGIAN DISHES TO TRY

**Mussels with Fries**[83]

## MOULES-FRITES (MUSSELS WITH FRIES)

A national favorite, mussels are typically steamed in white wine, herbs, garlic, or cream and served with a generous portion of **Belgian fries**. Enjoy this dish near the coast or in cities like **Brussels, Ghent, or Bruges**, where it's served in big pots with dipping sauces on the side.

## STOOFVLEES / CARBONNADE FLAMANDE (FLEMISH BEEF STEW)

This hearty, slow-cooked dish features **beef braised in dark beer**, often with onions and a touch of mustard or bread spread with mustard. It's deeply flavorful and usually served with fries or mashed potatoes.

## WATERZOOI

Originating from Ghent, waterzooi is a creamy stew made with either **chicken or fish**, vegetables, eggs, and cream. It's delicate, rich, and best enjoyed with crusty bread to soak up the broth.

## VOL-AU-VENT

A puff pastry shell filled with **creamy chicken, mushrooms**, and sometimes meatballs, this dish is pure Belgian comfort food. Served with mashed potatoes or fries, it's especially popular in brasseries.

## RABBIT WITH PRUNES (LAPIN AUX PRUNEAUX)

A specialty of **Wallonia**, this sweet and savory dish features **rabbit braised in a dark sauce made with beer or wine and prunes**. It's traditional, rustic, and often cooked for Sunday meals or family gatherings.

Waterzooi[84]

## BELGIUM'S FAMOUS FRITES

**A delicious frites serving**[85]

Don't call them "French fries" — Belgians take their **frites** very seriously. These thick-cut, double-fried potatoes are crispy on the outside, soft on the inside, and served in paper cones with a wide range of sauces.

### POPULAR SAUCE CHOICES INCLUDE:

- **Andalouse** – Tangy tomato and mayo blend
- **Samurai** – Spicy with chili and garlic
- **Curry ketchup** – A sweet-spicy twist
- **Classic mayonnaise** – Smooth and rich

Look for **friteries or fritkots**, the small stands that serve fries across the country. Some of the best are in **Brussels, Namur, and Leuven**.

# WAFFLES WORTH THE WAIT

**Traditional sugar waffles**

Belgium is home to **two main types of waffles**, and both are worth trying:

## BRUSSELS WAFFLE

- ✦ Light, crisp, and rectangular
- ✦ Usually served with powdered sugar, whipped cream, fruit, or chocolate
- ✦ Often found at cafes and restaurants

## LIÈGE WAFFLE

- ✦ Dense, chewy, and sweet
- ✦ Made with pearl sugar that caramelizes on the outside
- ✦ Best eaten hot from street vendors

Locals enjoy waffles as a snack or dessert—not usually for breakfast — so, don't be surprised to find them sold **on-the-go or at train stations**.

# CHOCOLATES AND SWEETS

## BELGIAN CHOCOLATE

**Mouth-watering Belgian chocolate**

Belgium is world-famous for its **high-quality chocolate**, made with **pure cocoa butter** and crafted with care.

### WELL-KNOWN CHOCOLATE HOUSES INCLUDE:

+ **Neuhaus** – Invented the Belgian filled praline

+ **Leonidas** – Affordable and accessible

+ **Pierre Marcolini** – Luxury, bean-to-bar craftsmanship

✦ **The Chocolate Line (in Bruges and Antwerp)** – Known for bold, artistic flavors

Visit chocolate shops to sample **handmade pralines, ganache, truffles, and chocolate bars**, or take a **chocolate-making workshop**.

## ALSO, TRY THE FOLLOWING DURING YOUR VISIT TO BELGIUM:

### SPECULOOS

A spiced shortcrust cookie traditionally eaten around Christmas but now available year-round. Try it plain, dipped in coffee, or as a **creamy cookie spread**.

A cuberdon cart om Ghent[86]

## CUBERDONS

A **cone-shaped raspberry candy**, often called "neuzekes" or "noses," popular in Ghent. They have a firm shell and gooey interior—sweet, nostalgic, and uniquely Belgian.

## BEER – BELGIUM'S LIQUID GOLD

Belgian beer served during an open air tasting

With over **1,500 varieties**, Belgium is a global capital of beer. Its brewing tradition stretches back centuries and includes **Trappist, abbey, lambic, saison, and strong golden ales**.

### TYPES OF BELGIAN BEER TO TRY:

- **Trappist Beers** – Brewed by monks in six Belgian abbeys (like Chimay, Orval, Westmalle)
- **Dubbel and Tripel** – Strong, dark or golden ales with fruity and spicy notes

- **Lambic and Gueuze** – Sour beers made with wild yeast, often blended and aged
- **Witbier** – Refreshing white beer brewed with citrus and coriander (e.g. Hoegaarden)

Beer is often **served in a specific glass designed for each brand**, and pairing beer with food is part of the culture. Don't hesitate to ask for a recommendation—**bartenders are often passionate experts**.

## WHERE TO ENJOY BELGIAN BEER:

- **Delirium Café (Brussels)** – World record for most beers available
- **De Dulle Griet (Ghent)** – Known for its strong beers and quirky shoe-deposit system
- **Brewery tours** – De Halve Maan in Bruges, De Koninck in Antwerp, or a Trappist abbey in Chimay or Westvleteren

*Scan the QR Code for an interactive map of Belgium breweries.*

## CHEESE AND CHARCUTERIE

Belgium also produces a variety of **local cheeses** such as:

- **Chimay** – Made by Trappist monks, washed rind
- **Passendale** – Soft, mild, and creamy
- **Herve** – A strong-smelling cheese from Wallonia
- **Orval** – Semi-soft and flavorful, made at Orval Abbey

Pair cheese with a Belgian beer, cured meats, and fresh bread for a perfect local picnic.

## VEGETARIAN AND MODERN CUISINE

Belgium is increasingly **vegetarian- and vegan-friendly**, especially in cities like **Ghent**, which introduced "Veggie Thursdays" across local schools and restaurants.

### YOU'LL FIND:

+ **Plant-based takes on classic dishes**
+ **Trendy veggie cafes** in Leuven, Antwerp, and Brussels
+ **Fusion flavors**—Belgium's colonial history and diverse population influence its food scene with **Moroccan, Congolese, and Southeast Asian cuisine** appearing on many menus

## FOOD MARKETS AND LOCAL EXPERIENCES

For authentic tastes and regional products, Belgium's towns and cities offer **vibrant markets, artisanal food fairs, and hands-on culinary experiences** that connect you to local life and flavor.

**The famous Vrijdagmarkt**

## EXPLORE:

- **Local markets in nearly every town** – These are perfect for sampling fresh produce, cheeses, meats, and breads. For example:
  - **Place du Jeu de Balle Flea Market in Brussels** (daily) – A excellent place to browse antiques.
  - **Vrijdagmarkt in Ghent** (Fridays & Saturdays) – Local farmers, butchers, and florists fill the square with color and smells
  - **Antwerp Exotic Market on Theaterplein** (Saturdays) – Offers olives, spices, world foods, and fresh juice stands
- **Artisan food fairs** – Held seasonally, often in castles, abbeys, or village squares. Look for events featuring:
  - **Walloon cheese tastings** (like Herve or Chimay)
  - **Trappist beer samplings** from abbeys including Orval and Rochefort
  - **Pastry and chocolate expos** such as the *Salon du Chocolat* in Brussels
  - **Honey, jams, and preserves** made from regional fruits, often available in Durbuy or the Ardennes

These experiences offer more than just food — they provide a **deeper connection to Belgium's culinary identity**, and often include storytelling, recipes, and personal insights from local hosts.

## DINING ETIQUETTE AND TIPS

- **Lunch is often the main meal**, with dinner eaten between 7–9 PM
- **Tipping is optional** but appreciated (rounding up or leaving 5–10% is common)
- **Tap water is safe to drink**, but many restaurants only serve bottled water
- **Reservations** are recommended for dinner in popular restaurants, especially on weekends

Belgian food is about pleasure, patience, and pride. Whether it's a simple cone of fries, a carefully brewed beer, or a hand-rolled praline, every bite tells a story of craftsmanship and culture. For travelers, the culinary journey through Belgium is as rich and rewarding as the landmarks themselves.

# CHAPTER 10
# BELGIUM FOR ADVENTURE SEEKERS

Belgium may be known for its history, waffles, and fairy-tale cities — but it also has plenty to offer travelers who crave action, exploration, and outdoor thrills. Thanks to its diverse landscapes, well-marked trails, and compact size, Belgium is ideal for both light outdoor activity and full-on adventure travel. Whether you're biking through forests, kayaking down rivers, or discovering caves, Belgium combines natural beauty with real excitement.

In this chapter, you'll find the best activities, regions, and adventure-friendly destinations for an **active, unforgettable escape**.

A traveler is seen hiking in Ardennes

## 1. CYCLING THROUGH FLANDERS AND BEYOND

Belgium is a **cycling country**, and it shows. With thousands of kilometers of dedicated bike routes, you can ride through **historic cities, countryside, coastal dunes, or forest trails**—all on safe, well-marked paths.

### BEST PLACES TO CYCLE:

+ **Flanders** – The flat north is perfect for casual riders. Explore scenic routes between **Ghent, Bruges, and Antwerp**, passing windmills, canals, and farmland.
+ **Tour of Flanders Route (Ronde van Vlaanderen)** – For seasoned cyclists, this route follows the path of the famous race, with steep cobbled climbs like **Oude Kwaremont and Paterberg** near Oudenaarde.
+ **Limburg** – Known as Belgium's most bike-friendly province, it offers routes like **Cycling Through Water** in Bokrijk—where your path cuts right through a lake.

### TIP:

Many cities offer **bike rental and sharing systems**, including Blue-bike (nationwide) and Villo! (Brussels).

*More information about Villo!*

## 2. HIKING IN THE ARDENNES

The **Ardennes**, in southern Belgium, is a rugged, forested region full of hiking trails for all skill levels. Expect peaceful woods, rolling hills, dramatic rock formations, and charming villages along the way.

### POPULAR HIKING AREAS:

+ **Semois Valley** – Near Bouillon, with trails along cliffs and riverbanks. Try the loop from **Rochehaut to Frahan** for panoramic views.

+ **Ninglinspo Trail** – Belgium's only mountain river trail, this 6-km path follows waterfalls and rocky streams—short, scenic, and great for families.

+ **High Fens (Hautes Fagnes)** – Belgium's highest plateau. Hike along **boardwalks through misty peat bogs and open heath**, especially beautiful in spring and fall.

Many trails are part of the **GR (Grande Randonnée) network**, with clear red and white waymarks.

## 3. KAYAKING AND CANOEING ON BELGIAN RIVERS

Belgium's rivers offer **calm water adventures with stunning scenery**, perfect for a summer day trip or weekend getaway.

Kayaking is a popular outdoor activity in Belgium[87]

## WHERE TO GO:

+ **Lesse River (Dinant region)** – Popular for family-friendly paddling, with routes ranging from 12 to 21 km. Pass by cliffs, caves, and castles.
+ **Ourthe River (La Roche-en-Ardenne)** – Ideal for beginners, with smooth currents and forested banks. Kayak rentals are easy to find.
+ **Semois River** – Offers a wilder, quieter paddle. Start from Bouillon or Alle-sur-Semois for remote and peaceful stretches.

### TIP:

Most kayaking is available from April to October, depending on water levels.

## 4. ROCK CLIMBING AND VIA FERRATA

If you're looking to scale cliffs, Belgium has natural and manmade sites for climbers of all skill levels.

**Freÿr Rocks**

## CLIMBING SPOTS:

- **Freÿr Rocks (near Dinant)** – The most famous natural climbing site in Belgium, offering limestone cliffs up to 120 meters tall. Routes are varied and scenic, with views over the Meuse River.
- **Rochers de Marche-les-Dames** – Near Namur, a historic military training area with climbing routes now open to the public.
- **Via Ferrata in Landelies** – A secured climbing route with metal rungs, ladders, and cables, offering a great introduction to mountain climbing with safety gear provided.

Several climbing areas require permits or insurance — check local guidelines or go with a licensed guide.

## 5. UNDERGROUND ADVENTURES: CAVING AND SPELEO TOURS

The limestone landscape in southern Belgium is full of **caves and grottos**, many open to the public and others accessible with trained guides.

## EXPLORE:

- **Caves of Han-sur-Lesse** – Walk through Belgium's most famous cave system, with dramatic chambers, underground rivers, and sound-and-light shows.
- **Caves of Remouchamps** – Includes a boat ride on an underground river—the longest such boat trip in Europe.
- **Speleo Tours (wild caving)** – For true adventurers, guided tours offer access to **uncharted cave routes**, with crawling, climbing, and rope work. Look for certified operators near Han, Rochefort, or Couvin.

# 6. WINTER SPORTS IN THE HIGH FENS

*Cross-country skiing is a popular winter sport in Belgium*

Belgium isn't known for ski resorts, but **when snow falls**, the **High Fens (Hautes Fagnes)** and **East Cantons** transform into winter playgrounds.

## WINTER ACTIVITIES INCLUDE:

- **Cross-country skiing** – Popular trails near **Baraque Michel and Botrange**, with rental equipment available
- **Snowshoe hiking** – Guided or self-guided along forest paths
- **Sledding** – Small family slopes in towns like **Ovifat and Spa**

Snow is never guaranteed, but it can be magical from **December to February**, especially after a good snowfall.

## 7. ADVENTURE PARKS AND ZIPLINING

Families and thrill-seekers can enjoy **treetop adventures**, ziplines, rope courses, and obstacle parks across the country.

### TOP CHOICES:

+ **Dinant Aventure** – Offers ziplining over cliffs, bridge crossings, and underground exploration

+ **Adventure Valley Durbuy** – Belgium's largest adventure park with climbing walls, rafting, tubing, and even an alpine coaster

+ **Forestia (Theux)** – Combines a wildlife park with tree courses and climbing areas for kids and adults

These parks are fun for all ages and offer both full-day activities and shorter adventure circuits.

# 8. SAILING, SURFING, AND SAND DUNES AT THE BELGIAN COAST

*The Belgian coast offers several opportunities to enjoy the outdoors*

The **North Sea coast** might be calm, but it's still a hub for **windsurfing, sailing, and sand dune trekking**.

## ADVENTURE OPTIONS INCLUDE:

- **Kite surfing in Oostduinkerke** or **Nieuwpoort**, where wind conditions are ideal
- **Beach sailing (sand yachting)**—a high-speed sport along wide beaches like De Panne
- **Dune hikes and nature walks** in protected coastal reserves such as **Zwin Nature Park**

Combine your beach adventure with a seafood lunch, and you've got the perfect day outdoors.

## TIPS FOR ADVENTURE TRAVELERS IN BELGIUM

+ **Weather can change quickly** — pack layers and rain protection
+ **Train access is good**, but some adventure areas are best reached by car
+ **Many outdoor centers offer gear rentals**, guided tours, and beginner instruction
+ **Insurance and reservations** may be required for certain sports like climbing or kayaking — check in advance
+ **Spring through early autumn** is the best time for most outdoor activities

## ADVENTURE, BELGIAN STYLE

Belgium may not have towering mountains or vast wilderness, but it offers **a wide variety of outdoor experiences in a small, easy-to-navigate country**. Whether you're chasing river rapids, exploring forest trails, or flying across a zipline, the country has a way of surprising you—one adventure at a time.

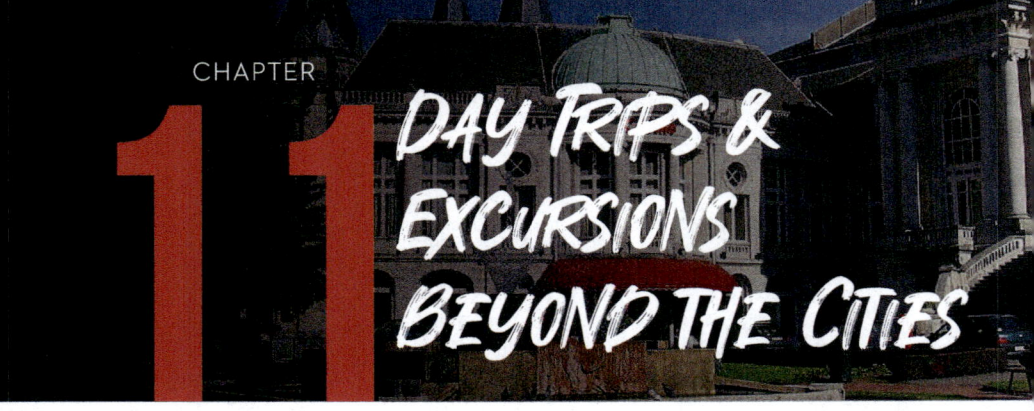

# CHAPTER 11
# DAY TRIPS & EXCURSIONS BEYOND THE CITIES

> **One of the best things about Belgium is how compact and well-connected it is. Thanks to high-speed trains, scenic roadways, and efficient public transport, you can explore castles, vineyards, abbeys, nature reserves, and even nearby countries — all in a single day.**

In this chapter, you'll discover **top day trips and excursions** from cities like Brussels, Bruges, Antwerp, and Ghent. These destinations offer **a break from the urban buzz**, while revealing even more of Belgium's rich history, landscapes, and local life.

People walking in the historic square of Mechelen[88]

## 1. LEUVEN – ACADEMIC CHARM AND BEER HERITAGE

**Distance from Brussels:** 25 minutes by train

Leuven is a **university city** full of youthful energy, historic architecture, and a long brewing tradition. Explore the **Gothic-style Town Hall**, relax in the **Botanic Garden**, and enjoy a drink at the **Oude Markt**, known as the "longest bar in the world."

## 2. WATERLOO BATTLEFIELD – HISTORY COMES ALIVE

**Distance from Brussels:** 45 minutes by car or train + local bus

The **Battle of Waterloo** (1815) was one of the most significant battles in European history, where **Napoleon Bonaparte was defeated**. Today, the site includes:

**Hougoumont Farm**[89]

- **Lion's Mound** – A man-made hill with sweeping views
- **Memorial 1815 Visitor Center** – Immersive museum experience with multimedia exhibits
- **Hougoumont Farm** – A key battle site restored with life-size displays It's a must for history lovers and a great family-friendly trip into Belgium's past. Scan the below QR Code for more information:

## 3. MECHELEN – SMALL, SCENIC, AND FULL OF SURPRISES

**Distance from Brussels or Antwerp:** 25 minutes by train

This often-overlooked gem is full of **historic charm, museums, and peaceful canals**. Climb **St. Rumbold's Tower** for panoramic views, explore the **Groot Begijnhof** (a UNESCO-listed former women's community), or take the kids to **Technopolis**, Belgium's science museum.

Mechelen blends **medieval calm with modern living**, and its compact size makes it easy to explore in a half or full day.

## 4. PAIRI DAIZA – BELGIUM'S PREMIER ANIMAL PARK

**Distance from Brussels:** 1 hour by car or train + shuttle

Voted one of the **best zoos in Europe**, **Pairi Daiza** is much more than a zoo—it's an immersive wildlife and garden experience set in a former monastery.

### HIGHLIGHTS INCLUDE:

- Giant pandas, elephants, gorillas, and snow leopards
- Themed worlds like **"The Kingdom of Ganesha"** and **"The Middle Kingdom"**
- On-site lodging for overnight stays among the animals

**Map view of Pairi Daiza**[90]

This setting is perfect for families, couples, and nature lovers.

*Scan the QR Code for more information.*

## 5. NAMUR – CASTLES, CLIFFS, AND RIVER VIEWS

**Distance from Brussels:** 1 hour by train

Set at the junction of the Meuse and Sambre rivers, **Namur** is the capital of **Wallonia** and a scenic destination known for its **citadel, river walks, and slow pace**. The **Citadel of Namur** offers guided tours and panoramic vistas, while the old town has cozy cafes, boutiques, and art galleries.

It's a relaxed day trip with a mix of **nature, history, and charm**.

# 6. ORVAL ABBEY – TRANQUILITY AND TRAPPIST BEER

Orval Abbey[91]

**Distance from Bouillon or southern Belgium:** 1–1.5 hours by car

Deep in the forested south, **Orval Abbey** is a working Trappist monastery known for its **world-famous beer and cheese**, made by the monks themselves. Visit the **ruins of the medieval abbey**, explore the modern church, and stop by the visitor center to learn about monastic life.

Pair your visit with a drive through the **Gaume region**, Belgium's "Little Provence," known for its sunny microclimate and peaceful villages.

## 7. SPA – THE ORIGINAL WELLNESS RETREAT

Spa's casino[92]

**Distance from Liège or Brussels:** 1.5–2 hours by train or car

The town of **Spa** gave its name to wellness centers worldwide. Today, it's still a destination for **relaxation and rejuvenation**. Visit the **Thermes de Spa** for thermal pools and saunas, stroll the **wooded hills of the Ardennes**, or try your luck at Belgium's oldest casino.

Pair your visit with nearby hikes or scenic drives through the **High Fens**.

# 8. HASSELT – FASHION, FLAVORS, AND JAPANESE GARDENS

**Het Borrelmanneke, seen at Hasselt**[93]

**Distance from Brussels:** 1 hour by train

Known for its **jenever (Belgian gin)** and designer boutiques, Hasselt is an easy-going city with a few standout attractions:

- **Japanese Garden** – One of the largest in Europe, peaceful in spring and autumn
- **Jenever Museum** – Learn about this traditional spirit and enjoy a tasting
- **Street art and fashion** – Creative energy flows through the city's stylish shops and murals

This is a perfect setting for a modern-day mix of **flavor, culture, and calm**.

## 9. DAY TRIPS ACROSS THE BORDER

Belgium's central location makes it easy to explore neighboring countries—**no passport checks within the Schengen zone**. Here are a few quick cross-border adventures:

- **Lille, France – 35 minutes by train from Brussels** A lively French city with Flemish charm, perfect for food, art, and boutique shopping.
- **Maastricht, Netherlands – 1.5 hours by train** One of the Netherlands' oldest cities, with Roman ruins, cozy cafes, and stylish shops.
- **Luxembourg City – 3 hours by train**
- A dramatic setting with fortresses, valleys, and a blend of French and German cultures.

## TIPS FOR PLANNING DAY TRIPS IN BELGIUM

- **Trains are fast and reliable**, with frequent service between cities
- **SNCB/NMBS rail passes** offer savings for multiple day trips
- **Pack comfortable walking shoes** — many destinations have cobbled streets
- Most museums and castles **close on Mondays**

- ✦ Book any **castle, spa, or abbey visits in advance**, especially in high season
- ✦ **Pair trips with local food**—each region has its own flavors and specialties

## EXPLORE MORE, STRESS LESS

With so many destinations just an hour or two away, Belgium makes it easy to **see more without rushing**. Day trips give you the chance to dive deeper into the country's **natural beauty, rural life, and rich heritage**, all while returning to your city base by evening.

# CHAPTER 12
# WHERE TO STAY – BEST AREAS & ACCOMMODATIONS

Finding the right place to stay can shape your entire trip. In Belgium, you'll find everything from elegant city hotels and cozy B&Bs to castle stays, boutique inns, and affordable hostels. The country's compact size also means you can stay in one city and take easy day trips to others — making it simple to mix comfort with convenience.

In this chapter, we'll break down the **best areas to stay in each major city**, plus options for countryside escapes and unique experiences.

People relax with a scenic view of Bruges Town Hall in Belgium[94]

# BEST PLACES TO STAY IN BRUSSELS

**Grand Place, Brussels**[95]

## 1. CITY CENTER (AROUND GRAND PLACE)

Best for first-time visitors who want to be close to top attractions like the Grand Place, Manneken Pis, and the Royal Palace. You'll find everything from **boutique hotels to luxury chains** here.

- **Good for:** Sightseeing, walking tours, nightlife
- **Stay here if:** You want to be in the heart of it all

## 2. IXELLES AND SAINT-GILLES

Trendy, artsy neighborhoods full of **local cafes, shops, and Art Nouveau architecture**. These areas offer a quieter, more local feel while still being close to the center.

- **Good for:** Food lovers, culture, longer stays
- **Stay here if:** You enjoy stylish, residential areas

## 3. EUROPEAN QUARTER

This area is home to EU institutions and modern hotels. It's quieter on weekends and ideal for business travelers or those looking for **parks and museums nearby**.

- ✦ **Good for:** Business travelers, peace and quiet
- ✦ **Stay here if:** You want clean, modern, and well-connected accommodations

## BEST PLACES TO STAY IN BRUGES

**Bruges Market Square**[96]

## 1. HISTORIC CITY CENTER (BINNENSTAD)

The most charming option, where you'll stay steps from canals, cobbled squares, and medieval buildings. Hotels here range from romantic inns to luxury guesthouses in **heritage buildings**.

- ✦ **Good for:** Couples, photographers, history buffs
- ✦ **Stay here if:** You want the full fairy-tale Bruges experience

## 2. SINT-ANNA QUARTER

Just outside the tourist center, this quiet area offers **peaceful B&Bs and budget-friendly stays**, with easy access to the city's main sights by foot or bike.

- ✦ **Good for:** Budget travelers, families
- ✦ **Stay here if:** You want value and calm surroundings

## BEST PLACES TO STAY IN GHENT

**An eye-catching historic building in Ghent**[97]

## 1. PATERSHOL AND CITY CENTER

Full of character, charm, and canal views. You'll be within walking distance of the **Gravensteen Castle, churches, and riverside cafés**.

- ✦ **Good for:** Sightseeing, couples, and boutique stays
- ✦ **Stay here if:** You love historic settings and nightlife nearby

## 2. ARTS QUARTER AND STATION AREA

Closer to **Ghent-Saint-Peter's Station**, this area is convenient for **day trips and public transport**. It's also home to museums and greener areas.

+ **Good for:** Train travelers, families, longer stays
+ **Stay here if:** You want space and easy access to transport

## BEST PLACES TO STAY IN ANTWERP

The interior of the Antwerp Museum[98]

## 1. HISTORIC CENTER (AROUND CATHEDRAL AND GROTE MARKT)

Perfect for visitors who want to explore **on foot**. This area is filled with **fashion boutiques, dining spots, and cultural sites**.

+ **Good for:** Short stays, first-timers, foodies
+ **Stay here if:** You love being close to museums, shops, and bars

## 2. ZUID DISTRICT (HET ZUID)

Trendy and artsy, with modern art galleries, cool cafes, and boutique hotels. It's popular with locals and creatives.

- **Good for:** Stylish travelers, art lovers
- **Stay here if:** You want a more local, contemporary vibe

## 3. CENTRAL STATION & DIAMOND DISTRICT

Convenient for travelers arriving by train, this area offers **larger hotels and better deals** while still being walkable to the city center.

- **Good for:** Budget-conscious travelers, business visitors
- **Stay here if:** You want easy access to transport and affordability

# COUNTRYSIDE & UNIQUE STAYS IN BELGIUM

Belgium's **countryside and small towns** offer **authentic, quiet escapes**, perfect for relaxing after days in the city.

## CASTLE HOTELS:

- **Château de la Poste (near Namur)** – A peaceful stay in a forested park
- **Manoir de Lébioles (Spa region)** – Luxury in the Ardennes with spa services
- **Château d'Hassonville (Wallonia)** – Elegant estate with fine dining and gardens

## RURAL B&BS AND FARM STAYS:

In Flanders and Wallonia, you'll find **charming guesthouses** offering home-cooked meals, local wine or beer, and often **direct access to hiking and biking trails**.

## TRAPPIST MONASTERY GUESTHOUSES:

While rare, some abbeys offer **quiet guest accommodations**, ideal for spiritual retreats or peaceful solo stays. Advance booking and respect for silence are essential.

## BUDGET-FRIENDLY OPTIONS

Belgium has many **affordable and clean hostels**, particularly in major cities:

- **MEININGER (Brussels and Ghent)** – Modern, well-rated, and central
- **Snuffel Hostel (Bruges)** – Great design and location
- **Boomerang Hostel (Antwerp)** – Simple and sociable

## ALSO CONSIDER:

- **Apartments and vacation rentals** – Ideal for families and longer stays
- **University housing** – Available in summer, especially in Leuven and Ghent

## BOOKING TIPS

- **Book early** for weekends and peak seasons (spring, summer, December)
- Many hotels offer **multi-night discounts** and breakfast packages
- Check for **city taxes** (charged per night, per person at check-out)
- In small towns, **check hours carefully**—reception may not be open all day
- Consider **staying near train stations** if you plan to take day trips

## SLEEP EASY, EXPLORE MORE

Whether you're dreaming of a **canal-side inn in Bruges**, a **design loft in Antwerp**, or a **castle in the countryside**, Belgium has a place for you to **rest, recharge, and wake up ready to explore**. With a little planning, you'll find accommodations that match your style, pace, and budget—**making your journey even more comfortable and memorable.**

# CHAPTER 13
# BELGIUM'S CULTURE, CUSTOMS & ETIQUETTE

Belgium is a country with deep traditions, strong regional identities, and a culture shaped by both history and diversity. While its people are friendly and welcoming, understanding a few local customs will help you connect more easily and travel with **confidence and respect**.

This chapter will guide you through **social etiquette, communication styles, cultural differences**, and tips for navigating daily life in Belgium like a local.

Puppets seen during a festival in Brussels[99]

# UNDERSTANDING BELGIUM'S REGIONAL CULTURES

Belgium is made up of **three regions**, each with its own language, identity, and traditions:

## FLANDERS (NORTHERN BELGIUM)

- **Language:** Dutch (Flemish dialect)
- **Culture:** Organized, industrious, and direct
- **Cities:** Brussels (partially), Bruges, Ghent, Antwerp, Leuven

## WALLONIA (SOUTHERN BELGIUM)

- **Language:** French
- **Culture:** Warm, relaxed, and family-oriented
- **Cities:** Namur, Liège, Dinant, Mons

## BRUSSELS CAPITAL REGION

- **Languages:** Officially bilingual (French and Dutch), but French is dominant
- **Culture:** International, diverse, and politically central

## GERMAN-SPEAKING COMMUNITY (EAST BELGIUM)

- **Language:** German
- **Small region** near the German border, with distinct traditions and governance

## TIP:

It's polite to **greet people in their native language**, especially in small towns. If unsure, English is widely understood in cities.

## GREETINGS AND COMMUNICATION

+ A **handshake** is the standard greeting in most settings—firm, brief, and with eye contact.

+ Among friends, **three cheek kisses (alternating sides)** are common in Wallonia; in Flanders, it's more reserved.

+ Titles matter: Use **"Monsieur" (Mr.) or "Madame" (Mrs.)** in French areas, and **"Meneer" or "Mevrouw"** in Dutch-speaking areas.

## COMMUNICATION STYLE:

+ Belgians tend to be **polite, formal, and reserved**, especially in professional or public settings.

+ They appreciate **modesty, punctuality,** and **well-structured conversations**.

+ Humor is subtle, and **being too loud or overly casual** in public is often frowned upon.

## DINING AND TABLE MANNERS

Belgium takes pride in **quality food and drink**, and dining is often a relaxed but respectful experience.

People enjoy a seaside meal in Knokke-Heist[100]

## TABLE ETIQUETTE:

- **Wait to be seated**—don't take a table without asking, especially in cafes.
- It's common to **keep hands on the table (not on your lap)**, but not elbows.
- Say **"bon appétit"** (French) or **"smakelijk"** (Dutch) before eating.
- **Finish all food** on your plate—it's considered respectful.
- **Tipping** is not expected, but appreciated—rounding up or leaving 5-10% is typical.

## DINING OUT:

- **Dinner is the biggest meal of the day**, usually served between 7-9 PM.
- **Tap water is safe to drink**, but many restaurants only serve **bottled water**.
- In casual settings, **splitting the bill is common** among younger Belgians.

## PUNCTUALITY AND DAILY LIFE

- Belgians are generally **punctual**, especially in business and formal settings.
- For social events, a **5-10 minute delay** is usually fine, but arriving early is not expected.
- **Shops often close early**, especially in small towns. Many businesses close on Sundays and Monday mornings.

## DRESS CODE AND APPEARANCE

Belgians dress **neatly and conservatively**, especially in cities. Even casual outfits are typically **clean, stylish, and coordinated**.

## FOR TRAVELERS:

- **Smart casual** is ideal for most situations.
- **Beachwear is for the beach only**—avoid wearing swimsuits in town centers or restaurants.
- In religious buildings (like churches and abbeys), dress **modestly and quietly**—cover shoulders and remove hats.

## LOCAL CUSTOMS AND SOCIAL NORMS

### RESPECT FOR PRIVACY:

Belgians are polite but value personal space and privacy. Avoid asking personal questions unless invited.

### RECYCLING AND CLEANLINESS:

Belgians take recycling and littering seriously. You'll find **separate bins for paper, plastic, and glass**, and there are fines for littering or improper sorting.

### SUNDAY QUIET:

Many neighborhoods and small towns treat Sundays as **quiet family days**. Lawn mowing, loud music, and heavy chores are discouraged. Plan accordingly—shops may be closed or have reduced hours.

## CULTURAL CELEBRATIONS AND TRADITIONS

An Ommegang celebration[101]

- **Carnival (February/March):** Wallonia is famous for colorful celebrations, especially in Binche (UNESCO-listed).
- **Ommegang (July):** A medieval pageant in Brussels' Grand Place.
- **Christmas Markets (December):** Bruges, Ghent, and Brussels transform into winter wonderlands.
- **National Day (July 21):** Celebrates the inauguration of Belgium's first king in 1831 with parades and fireworks.
- **Beer and Food Festivals:** Held year-round across regions to celebrate local specialties.

## LANGUAGE TIPS & PHRASES

Even though many Belgians speak English, learning a few local words is appreciated.

### IN DUTCH (FLEMISH):
- Hello: Hallo
- Please: Alsjeblieft
- Thank you: Dank u
- Goodbye: Tot ziens
- Do you speak English?: Spreekt u Engels?

### IN FRENCH (WALLONIA & BRUSSELS):
- Hello: Bonjour
- Please: S'il vous plaît
- Thank you: Merci
- Goodbye: Au revoir
- Do you speak English?: Parlez-vous anglais?

### TIP:
Always **start a conversation with a greeting** even if just entering a shop. It's considered rude to launch straight into a question.

## WHAT MAKES BELGIAN CULTURE SPECIAL

Belgian culture is a **blend of influences**, shaped by its history, language diversity, and position at the heart of Europe. Despite regional differences, Belgians share a love for **good food, strong community ties, and a balanced lifestyle**.

Travelers who show **respect, curiosity, and a willingness to adapt** are often welcomed with warm hospitality, local stories, and maybe even a surprise chocolate or beer recommendation.

## A CULTURE OF SUBTLE RICHNESS

Belgium doesn't shout to be noticed. Instead, it invites you to look a little closer—to admire a carved doorway, savor a slow-cooked meal, or appreciate a centuries-old custom still alive today.

By understanding the **rhythms of daily life, local manners, and cultural values**, you'll not only travel better—you'll experience Belgium in the way it's meant to be lived: **with quiet appreciation and genuine connection.**

# CHAPTER 14
# UNDERSTANDING BELGIUM'S CURRENCY & MONEY MATTERS

Money might not be the most exciting part of your trip—but understanding how payments work in Belgium will help you save time, avoid extra fees, and travel more confidently. Belgium is modern and efficient when it comes to money, but there are still a few important things to know before you go.

This chapter gives you a **simple, practical overview** of Belgium's currency, how to pay, where to exchange, and what to expect at shops, restaurants, and hotels.

**A colorful shop situated in Brussels**[102]

Making shopping in Belgium easy – have a look below at our top tips[103]

## WHAT CURRENCY IS USED IN BELGIUM?

Belgium uses the **euro (€)**, the official currency of the European Union.

- **Currency code:** EUR
- **Common bills:** €5, €10, €20, €50, €100
- **Common coins:** 1, 2, 5, 10, 20, 50 cents + €1, €2

> **TIP:**
>
> Carry some **small coins**, especially for public toilets, vending machines, and market stalls.

## PAYING IN BELGIUM – CASH OR CARD?

### Card Payments

Credit and debit cards are widely accepted in Belgium, especially in cities. Most places accept:

+ **Visa**
+ **Mastercard**
+ **Maestro / Bancontact** (local debit system)

**Contactless payments** and **mobile wallets** (Apple Pay, Google Pay) are becoming common, especially in larger stores and restaurants.

### Cash Payments

Cash is still used in many smaller shops, **rural areas**, **markets**, and for tipping. Always have a bit of cash on hand, especially for:

+ Farmers' markets
+ Bakeries and small cafés
+ Public transport ticket machines
+ Local bars or friteries (fries stands)

## CURRENCY EXCHANGE TIPS

+ **Best exchange rate:** Withdraw euros from an ATM using your debit card.
+ **Avoid airport kiosks**—they often offer poor rates and high fees.
+ **Bank branches** offer currency exchange but may charge service fees.
+ **Bring a backup card**, especially if your main card doesn't work or is declined.

### TIP:

Let your bank know you're traveling to avoid blocked transactions.

## USING ATMS IN BELGIUM

ATMs (**"Geldautomaat"**) are widely available and easy to use.

+ Most offer **multiple language options**, including English.
+ Look for machines near banks or train stations for the best security.
+ Use ATMs **attached to banks**, not freestanding ones in tourist zones (which may charge extra).
+ Belgian ATMs usually **do not charge local withdrawal fees**, but your bank might.

## TIPPING IN BELGIUM

Tipping is not required, but it's appreciated in certain situations:

| SERVICE | TIPPING ETIQUETTE |
|---|---|
| Restaurants | Not expected. Round up or leave 5-10% for good service. |
| Cafés & Bars | Round up to the nearest euro |
| Taxis | Optional—round up or add a euro or two |
| Hotel Staff | A couple of euros for bellhops or housekeeping |
| Tour Guides | €2-€5 per person for group tours, more for private |

## TAXES AND VAT REFUNDS

Belgium's sales tax (**VAT**) is already included in prices—so no surprises at checkout.

+ **Standard VAT:** 21% on most goods and services
+ **Reduced VAT:** 6-12% for books, food, and transportation

## FOR NON-EU TRAVELERS:

If you spend **€125 or more** in a single store in one day, you may be eligible for a **VAT refund** when leaving the EU.

## HOW TO CLAIM:

1. Ask for a **VAT refund form** at the store when you buy.
2. Present the form, receipt, goods, and passport at customs when departing the EU.
3. Get the refund via cash, card credit, or service provider (e.g., Global Blue).

**Note:** Not all shops offer this — look for **"Tax-Free Shopping"** signs or ask in advance.

## OTHER HELPFUL TIPS

+ **Split bills?** Often possible, but ask politely—especially in small restaurants.
+ **Public toilets** may charge **€0.50–€1**, usually cash only.
+ **Service charges** are included in prices—there's no need to tip extra unless you wish to.
+ **Be discreet with cash and valuables**, especially in crowded areas or stations.

## QUICK SUMMARY

| ITEM | DETAILS |
|---|---|
| Currency | Euro (€) |
| Card Use | Widely accepted, including contactless |
| Cash Needed | For small purchases, local markets, tips |
| ATMs | Easy to find, usually no local fees |
| Tipping | Modest, optional |
| VAT Refund | Possible for non-EU visitors on €125+ spend |

Understanding how money works in Belgium will help you **shop, dine, and travel with ease**. With a little preparation, you can spend more time enjoying your journey—and less time worrying about the bill.

CHAPTER

# 15

## SEASONAL EVENTS & FESTIVITIES

> Belgium may be small, but its calendar is packed with colorful festivals, historic parades, and joyful seasonal traditions that bring streets, squares, and villages to life. From ancient folklore to modern music festivals, Belgians know how to celebrate—and visitors are always welcome to join in.

This chapter takes you through **Belgium's major seasonal events**, so you can plan your trip around **local traditions, cultural highlights, and unforgettable moments**.

**Gentse Feesten**[104]

# SPRING (MARCH - MAY)

## FLORALIA BRUSSELS

**Where:** Groot-Bijgaarden Castle (near Brussels)

**When:** April – early May

Thousands of tulips, hyacinths, and daffodils bloom across 14 hectares of landscaped gardens. The flower displays are breathtaking, and the castle backdrop adds fairytale charm.

## HALLERBOS BLUEBELL SEASON

**Where:** Hallerbos Forest, near Halle

**When:** Mid-April – early May

The forest floor transforms into a **carpet of blooming bluebells**, attracting nature lovers and photographers from across Europe. The best blooms last just a few weeks, so timing is everything.

## ZYTHOS BEER FESTIVAL

**Where:** Leuven

**When:** April

Belgium's largest consumer beer festival brings together over 100 breweries and hundreds of craft beers. Entry includes a glass and tokens to taste.

## SUMMER (JUNE - AUGUST)

### OMMEGANG PAGEANT

**Where:** Brussels

**When:** Early July

A grand historical reenactment held in the **Grand Place**, this festival features **costumed parades, knights on horseback, and traditional music,** recreating the 1549 visit of Charles V. It's like stepping into a living Renaissance painting.

### GENTSE FEESTEN (GHENT FESTIVAL)

**Where:** Ghent

**When:** Mid-July (10 days)

Ghent's city center turns into one big open-air festival with **live music, theater, street performers, food stalls, and fireworks**. It's one of Europe's largest cultural festivals and a must-see if you're visiting in July.

## TOMORROWLAND

**Where:** Boom, between Brussels and Antwerp

**When:** Late July

A world-famous **electronic music festival**, Tomorrowland draws fans from all over the world. Tickets sell out fast, but even if you can't attend, the energy in nearby towns is contagious.

## DUCASSE D'ATH (GIANTS PARADE)

**Where:** Ath (Wallonia)

**When:** August

UNESCO-recognized, this traditional festival features **giant puppets parading through town**, reenacting medieval stories. It's colorful, historic, and truly unique to Belgium.

# AUTUMN (SEPTEMBER – NOVEMBER)

## OPEN MONUMENT DAY

**Where:** Nationwide

**When:** Second weekend of September

Hundreds of historic buildings — castles, abbeys, private homes, and hidden sites — open their doors for **free public tours**. It's a fantastic way to see inside places usually closed to visitors.

## BRUSSELS DESIGN SEPTEMBER

**Where:** Brussels

**When:** All September

A month-long celebration of **Belgian and international design**, with exhibitions, pop-ups, tours, and creative events across the city. Perfect for art and architecture lovers.

## BEER FESTIVALS

- **BXLBeerFest (Brussels)** – A craft beer-focused event in early September
- **Modeste Beer Festival (Antwerp)** – Celebrating small, independent breweries

## FÊTE DE LA WALLONIE

**Where:** Namur

**When:** Mid-September

Wallonia's regional holiday is marked by **folk dancing, fireworks, concerts**, and plenty of local food and beer.

# WINTER (DECEMBER - FEBRUARY)

## CHRISTMAS MARKETS

**Where:** Brussels, Bruges, Ghent, Liège, and smaller towns

**When:** Late November - early January

Belgium's Christmas markets are full of **twinkling lights, handmade gifts, spiced wine, and festive foods**. Highlights include:

+ **Winter Wonders (Brussels)** – Belgium's biggest market with a Ferris wheel and skating rink
+ **Bruges Christmas Market** – Fairytale setting with cozy stalls and canals
+ **Liège's Village de Noël** – The oldest and largest in Wallonia

## BINCHE CARNIVAL

**Where:** Binche (Wallonia)

**When:** February or March (ends on Shrove Tuesday)

This UNESCO-listed event features **Gilles — costumed figures in wax masks and feathered hats — throwing oranges into the crowd** to bring good luck. It's one of Belgium's most fascinating and ancient traditions.

## LICHTFESTIVAL (LIGHT FESTIVAL)

**Where:** Ghent (every 3 years; check schedule)

**When:** Usually in February

The city becomes an open-air gallery of **light installations and projections**, created by artists from around the world. It's dazzling, interactive, and perfect for winter nights.

## NATIONAL HOLIDAYS & OBSERVANCES

- **Easter (March/April)** – Family time with church services, egg hunts, and chocolate gifts
- **Labor Day – May 1** – Public holiday; expect closures
- **Belgian National Day – July 21** – Parades, concerts, and fireworks across the country
- **All Saints' Day – November 1** – A quiet day for remembering loved ones, often marked by visits to cemeteries

## TIPS FOR ENJOYING EVENTS IN BELGIUM

- **Book accommodations early**—festivals often bring crowds and limited availability
- **Use public transportation**—cities provide extra services during major events
- **Pack for changing weather**, especially during spring and autumn festivals
- Check local **event calendars and city websites** for the most current dates and details
- Many events are **free or low-cost**, but some (like Tomorrowland) require advance tickets

## CELEBRATE LIKE A LOCAL

Belgian festivals offer a window into the country's **spirit, history, and creativity**. Whether you're dancing at a street party, sipping mulled wine in a winter market, or watching giants parade through a village square, these events bring people together in joyful, unforgettable ways.

CHAPTER

# 16

# SHOPPING & SOUVENIRS

> Whether you're wandering through open-air markets, browsing historic shopping galleries, or stepping into a family-run chocolate shop, Belgium is full of unique items worth taking home. From edible delights like pralines and beer to handcrafted lace and comic books, Belgian souvenirs tell a story — and many are made with the same attention to quality that defines the country's culture.

In this chapter, you'll find the **best souvenirs to buy**, **where to shop**, and **tips for bringing home authentic Belgian treasures**.

People seen shopping in Leuven[105]

# TOP BELGIAN SOUVENIRS TO TAKE HOME

## 1. BELGIAN CHOCOLATE

**A chocolate store seen in Bruges**[106]

Belgium is world-renowned for its **premium-quality chocolate**. Handcrafted pralines, truffles, and chocolate bars make thoughtful (and delicious) gifts.

### Top chocolate brands to try:

- **Neuhaus** – Inventor of the filled praline
- **Leonidas** – Affordable and widely available
- **Pierre Marcolini** – High-end, bean-to-bar creations
- **The Chocolate Line** – Artistic and bold, especially in Bruges and Antwerp
- **Galler** – Royal warrant holder, known for rich flavor and creative packaging

### TIP:

Buy from **boutique chocolatiers** for the freshest experience. Many offer boxes you can customize.

## 2. BELGIAN BEER

With over **1,500 varieties**, Belgian beer is a favorite souvenir for beer lovers. Each type comes with its **own unique glass**, making it a collectible item.

### Popular beer styles and brands:

- **Trappist beers** – Chimay, Orval, Westmalle
- **Lambic & Gueuze** – Cantillon, Boon, Lindemans
- **Strong ales** – Duvel, Delirium Tremens, La Chouffe
- **Witbier (white beer)** – Hoegaarden

You can also buy **gift packs** that include a mix of beers and matching glasses.

**Note:** Check airline rules for packing liquids, and consider purchasing at the **airport duty-free** if you're tight on space.

## 3. HANDMADE LACE

**Beautiful lace souveniers**

Belgium—especially Bruges—is famous for its **delicate, handwoven lace**, used in everything from table linens to clothing.

+ Look for **certified handmade items**, not mass-produced machine lace.
+ Bruges has many **lace workshops and museums** where you can see artisans at work.
+ Ideal gifts: lace bookmarks, doilies, handkerchiefs, or framed pieces.

## 4. BELGIAN COMICS & COLLECTIBLES

A scene from Tintin at the Brussels' Comics Art Museum[107]

Belgium is the birthplace of iconic comic characters like **Tintin, The Smurfs, Lucky Luke, and Spirou**. Comic books, figurines, and posters make fun souvenirs for all ages.

+ Visit **Brussels' Comics Art Museum** or **local comic shops** for French/Dutch and English editions.
+ Look for collectibles featuring **Hergé's Tintin**, including replica models, pins, and bags.

*More information about the Brussels' Comics Art Museum*

## 5. SPECULOOS AND SWEET TREATS

These **spiced cookies** are traditionally eaten around the holidays but are available year-round in shops and supermarkets.

### Other sweet options include:

- **Cuberdons (Ghent)** – Cone-shaped raspberry candies with soft centers
- **Belgian waffles** – Pre-packaged versions make tasty travel gifts
- **Pralines** – Often sold in beautiful gift boxes

## 6. BELGIAN LINEN, CERAMICS, AND DESIGN GOODS

Belgium has a growing reputation for **home goods, fashion, and contemporary design**. Look for:

- **Belgian linen** (napkins, tablecloths, scarves) in boutique shops
- **Artisanal ceramics** from local studios
- **Minimalist Belgian fashion** in Antwerp and Brussels, featuring local designers
- **Vintage shops** and **flea markets** for antiques and quirky finds

## WHERE TO SHOP IN BELGIUM

### BRUSSELS

- **Galeries Royales Saint-Hubert** – A historic shopping arcade with chocolatiers, luxury boutiques, and cafes
- **Rue Neuve** – Belgium's busiest shopping street with high-street fashion brands
- **Sablon District** – Antique shops, chocolate boutiques, and weekend markets
- **Place du Jeu de Balle** – A daily flea market full of second-hand treasures

## BRUGES

- **Steenstraat and Zuidzandstraat** – Lined with local shops, lace stores, and chocolate makers
- **Katelijnestraat** – Ideal for food, lace, and small artisan shops
- **Choco-Story & Lace Museum gift shops** – Offer curated items made locally

## ANTWERP

- **Meir** – High-end fashion and Belgian designers in a grand shopping boulevard
- **Nationalestraat** – Known for Belgian fashion and concept stores
- **Kloosterstraat** – Popular for antiques, interior design, and vintage finds

## GHENT

- **Veldstraat** – Central shopping street with a mix of fashion and Belgian brands
- **Patershol & Friday Market (Vrijdagmarkt)** – Local designers, food markets, and handmade goods
- **Local chocolate shops and comic stores** scattered throughout the old town

## LOCAL MARKETS WORTH VISITING

- **Antwerp Exotische Markt (Saturdays)** – International flavors, spices, and fresh produce
- **Brussels Midi Market (Sundays)** – Massive, lively, and full of bargains
- **Ghent's Bij Sint-Jacobs flea market (weekends)** – Great for books, antiques, and vintage items
- **Bruges Fish Market & Wednesday market** – Local delicacies, flowers, and crafts

## TIPS FOR SMART SHOPPING IN BELGIUM

+ **Shops often close early (6–7 PM)** and are usually closed on **Sundays and holidays**, except in tourist zones or special events.
+ **Tax-free shopping** may be available for non-EU residents—ask for a tax refund form at the register.
+ **Credit cards** are widely accepted, but some small markets prefer **cash**.
+ Always check **"Made in Belgium" labels** to ensure authenticity.

## BRING BELGIUM HOME WITH YOU

Whether you're sipping Trappist beer, tasting handmade chocolates, or framing a lace piece from Bruges, your Belgian souvenirs will carry the spirit of your travels long after you return home. These special items reflect the **craftsmanship, flavor, and creativity** that Belgium is known for.

# CHAPTER 17
## MOST RECOMMENDED SPOTS BY TRAVELERS

> Belgium may be compact, but it's filled with standout destinations and memorable experiences that leave a lasting impression. These are the places that visitors return to time and time again, not just because they're beautiful—but because they offer something distinctively Belgian.

This chapter explores the **top must-visit spots**, each offering a unique combination of history, scenery, architecture, or atmosphere that makes it truly special.

**Hallerbos**

## 1. ROZENHOEDKAAI, BRUGES

Often considered the **most picturesque corner of Bruges**, Rozenhoedkaai is where the city's iconic canal, gabled houses, and weeping willows come together in a single view. This serene spot captures the fairy-tale charm of Bruges and is especially beautiful at sunrise and sunset, when the water reflects the surrounding architecture in golden light.

## 2. BELFRY OF GHENT

Rising above the historic center, the **Belfry of Ghent** is a UNESCO-listed medieval tower that symbolizes the city's independence. Its location—between Saint Bavo's Cathedral and Saint Nicholas' Church—forms Ghent's famous skyline. The tower offers panoramic views from the top and houses one of the most important **carillons** (bell instruments) in Belgium, still played today.

## 3. GRAND PLACE, BRUSSELS

The **Grand Place** is Brussels' most iconic square, surrounded by **ornately decorated guildhalls, the Town Hall**, and the **Maison du Roi**. It is a masterpiece of 17th-century architecture and serves as a central location for festivals, concerts, and ceremonies. Its appearance changes with the seasons, from the vibrant **Flower Carpet** in summer to twinkling lights during winter markets.

## 4. ATOMIUM, BRUSSELS

A one-of-a-kind structure, the **Atomium** was built for the 1958 World's Fair and remains a symbol of post-war optimism and innovation. Designed as an iron crystal magnified 165 billion times, its nine interconnected spheres house exhibitions, an observation deck, and even a panoramic restaurant. It blends **futuristic design with interactive experiences**, making it popular for families and architecture fans alike.

## 5. CHÂTEAU DE BOUILLON

Overlooking the Semois River in the Ardennes, **Château de Bouillon** is one of Belgium's best-preserved medieval castles. It once belonged to Godfrey of Bouillon, a leader of the First Crusade. Visitors can explore its **ramparts, tunnels, towers, and dungeons**, as well as enjoy falconry demonstrations and sweeping forest views. The surrounding town and valley make this a perfect blend of history and nature.

## 6. GHENT'S NIGHTTIME LIGHT PLAN

Ghent's city center comes alive after dark thanks to a **city-wide lighting design**, known as the "Light Plan." Historic buildings, bridges, and canals are artistically lit to highlight their features without overwhelming them. A self-guided **night walk** reveals a completely different mood—peaceful, elegant, and cinematic.

## 7. OUDE MARKT, LEUVEN

Nicknamed the **"longest bar in the world,"** Leuven's Oude Markt is a large square lined with dozens of terrace cafes and bars. Located in the heart of a lively university city, it's a central gathering point that offers a vibrant social atmosphere. The square also features **historic facades, student energy, and year-round events**, from music to open-air dining.

## 8. MEUSE RIVER CRUISE, DINANT

A boat ride along the **Meuse River** offers a peaceful way to experience the natural beauty and historic architecture of Dinant and its surroundings. The **steep cliffs, citadels, and riverside abbeys** make this part of Wallonia especially scenic. Cruises range from short loops to longer scenic journeys through the valley, often with commentary highlighting the region's military and religious past.

## 9. HALLERBOS FOREST DURING BLUEBELL SEASON

Each spring, the **Hallerbos** forest near Halle bursts into bloom with millions of wild bluebells. For a few weeks in April, the forest floor is transformed into a **vibrant purple-blue carpet**, creating one of Belgium's most magical natural scenes. Quiet walking paths wind through tall beech trees, making this a popular seasonal destination for nature lovers and photographers.

## 10. STREET WAFFLES – BRUSSELS & LIÈGE

Belgium's waffles are world-famous, and trying one fresh from a **street vendor** is an essential experience. Two main types dominate:

+ **Brussels waffles** – light, rectangular, and often topped with whipped cream, fruit, or chocolate
+ **Liège waffles** – dense, sweet, and caramelized, with pearl sugar for crunch

Served warm and handheld, they're available at food stalls, bakeries, and train stations, making them the perfect on-the-go treat.

## 11. BRUGES CANAL BOAT TOUR

Bruges is often called the **Venice of the North**, and a **canal boat tour** offers a unique view of the city's hidden courtyards, stone bridges, and gardens. These guided rides provide a relaxing overview of Bruges' history and architecture in just 30 minutes, making it a great introduction for first-time visitors.

## 12. SAINT BAVO'S CATHEDRAL AND THE GHENT ALTARPIECE

Located in the heart of Ghent, **Saint Bavo's Cathedral** is a stunning Gothic structure that houses one of the world's most important artworks: **The Adoration of the Mystic Lamb** by the Van Eyck brothers. This 15th-century altarpiece is renowned for its detail, symbolism, and significance in art history. Modern digital displays in the visitor center help bring its story to life.

## 13. DELIRIUM CAFÉ, BRUSSELS

Known for holding the world record for **most beers available**, Delirium Café in Brussels is a paradise for beer enthusiasts. The menu includes over **2,000 varieties**, from Trappist classics to international rarities. It's located just off the Grand Place and features a cozy, rustic interior filled with brewer memorabilia.

## 14. LEUVEN TOWN HALL

An architectural masterpiece of **Gothic design**, the **Leuven Town Hall** is famed for its intricate facade, decorated with **over 200 statues** of local figures, scholars, and saints. Built in the 15th century, it stands as a symbol of Leuven's academic and cultural legacy. Guided tours reveal the building's ornate interiors and historical significance.

## 15. PAIRI DAIZA WILDLIFE PARK

Located in Brugelette, Wallonia, **Pairi Daiza** is one of Europe's top-rated zoos and nature parks. It spans themed gardens, historic architecture, and spacious habitats for animals from all over the world. Highlights include **giant pandas, elephants, tigers, and underwater viewing areas**, as well as on-site lodging options where guests can stay near the animals.

## 16. ANTWERP CENTRAL STATION

More than just a transit hub, **Antwerp Central Station** is often ranked among the most beautiful train stations in the world. Its grand **neo-Baroque dome, marble hallways, and ornate ironwork** make it a destination in its own right. The station connects the city to major European destinations and serves as a stunning welcome to Antwerp.

Belgium's top spots are more than just beautiful — they're full of **character, story, and authenticity**. Whether you're taking in a sweeping river view, climbing a centuries-old tower, or enjoying a local snack in a bustling square, these recommended experiences help capture the **true essence of Belgian travel**.

CHAPTER

# 18

# THE 20 BEST PHOTO SPOTS IN BELGIUM

> **Belgium is packed with photogenic places, from medieval towers to modern architecture, fairy-tale towns to forested trails. This chapter features 20 of the best photo spots in Belgium, plus practical tips to help you capture each location at its most beautiful.**

Whether you're an amateur or seasoned photographer, Belgium offers unforgettable backdrops and frame-worthy moments at every turn.

Ghent[109]

176 | BELGIUM TRAVEL GUIDE

## PHOTOGRAPHY TIPS BEFORE YOU START

+ **Golden Hour = Magic Hour**

    Shoot during **sunrise or sunset** for softer light, longer shadows, and golden tones—especially in cities and countryside settings.

+ **Use Reflections**

    Belgium's canals, rivers, and wet cobblestones are perfect for capturing **mirror-like reflections**, especially in the early morning when water is still.

+ **Go Vertical for Towers & Architecture**

    Many of Belgium's historic buildings are tall and narrow — **vertical (portrait) shots** often frame them better.

+ **Pack for the Weather**

    Belgium can be cloudy or rainy. A **lens cloth, weather-sealed camera, or phone protection** goes a long way.

+ **Respect the Space**

    Many sites are **places of worship or private property**. Use zoom lenses or step back instead of entering restricted areas.

+ **Smartphone Tip:**

    Use **HDR mode** for landscapes, and **tap to focus** on your subject—especially in low light.

## TOP 20 PHOTO SPOTS IN BELGIUM

### 1. GRAND PLACE – BRUSSELS

A UNESCO World Heritage site, the square's **golden facades and Gothic details** are stunning from any angle. For best results, shoot at **dusk when lights begin to glow**, or during special events like the **Flower Carpet (August)**.

## 2. ROZENHOEDKAAI – BRUGES

This bend in the canal is **Bruges' most iconic view**, with reflections of medieval buildings and the Belfry in the water. Early morning and golden hour offer the softest light. A **wide-angle lens** works well here.

## 3. ATOMIUM – BRUSSELS

Photograph from below for dramatic perspective, or catch it **lit up at night**. Reflections from the metal spheres add depth. Try **framing it with trees** from the nearby park for added scale.

## 4. CHÂTEAU DE BOUILLON – ARDENNES

The castle on a cliff above the Semois River looks incredible from below or across the valley. Bring a **zoom lens** to capture detail in the stonework or falconry displays.

## 5. ST. MICHAEL'S BRIDGE – GHENT

This is **the best spot to capture Ghent's three towers** in one frame. Shoot toward the bridge in the evening for golden skies, or from the bridge for sweeping city views.

## 6. HALLERBOS FOREST – BLUEBELL SEASON

Visit in **mid to late April** for carpets of bluebells under beech trees. **Overcast light works best** to capture the flower colors. Stay on the trails and use a **lower angle** for magical forest floor shots.

## 7. BELFRY OF BRUGES – ROOFTOP VIEW

Climb the Belfry for a **panoramic view of Bruges'** rooftops and canals. Go early to avoid crowds and window glare. Use a **polarizing filter** if shooting through glass.

## 8. MEUSE RIVER – DINANT

Stand across the river to frame **the Church of Our Lady, colorful houses, and the citadel** on the cliff. Shoot during **blue hour (just after sunset)** for stunning reflections.

## 9. DURBUY – WALLONIA

Belgium's smallest city is full of narrow alleys, stone homes, and seasonal flowers. Focus on **textures and architectural details** for cozy, village-style shots.

## 10. BRUGES CANAL BOAT TOUR

Boat rides offer **low angles and unique perspectives**. Sit near the edges for the clearest views, and keep your shutter speed high to avoid blur from movement.

## 11. PAIRI DAIZA – BRUGELETTE

Great for both **wildlife and landscape photography**, especially in the themed gardens. Use **long lenses** for animal close-ups, and visit early or late to avoid crowds.

## 12. LEUVEN TOWN HALL

This ornate Gothic building is packed with carved detail. For best results, shoot at **an angle** to capture depth, or wait for **nightfall** when it's dramatically lit.

## 13. ANTWERP CENTRAL STATION

One of the world's most beautiful stations. Shoot from the main hall for symmetry, or go up a level for a **dramatic view down to the platforms**. Use a tripod for low-light shots indoors.

## 14. GRAND-HORNU – MONS

A UNESCO-listed industrial complex turned art center, it offers **bold shapes, shadows, and minimalist lines**—perfect for modern and architectural photography.

## 15. ZWIN NATURE PARK – KNOKKE-HEIST

Belgium's coastal wetlands are perfect for **wildlife and bird photography**, especially at dawn. Bring a **zoom lens and tripod**, and wear muted clothing to blend in.

### 16. MONT DES ARTS – BRUSSELS

A hilltop garden with a picture-perfect **view of the city center and spires**. Go at sunset for glowing cityscapes, or blue hour when streetlights begin to twinkle.

### 17. FLEMISH ARDENNES – EAST FLANDERS

Rolling hills, quiet villages, and farmland provide **classic rural Belgian scenery**. Sunrise fog, spring flowers, and winding cycling paths make it ideal for **landscape photography**.

### 18. GROTTE DE HAN – HAN-SUR-LESSE

Photograph dramatic **underground chambers** and stalactites. Use a **camera with low-light capabilities or a phone in night mode**. A small flashlight or headlamp can help with setup.

### 19. LIÈGE-GUILLEMINS TRAIN STATION

A striking modern design with white curves and vast skylights. Shoot from the inside for **symmetry and leading lines**, or outside at night for futuristic lighting.

### 20. CHRISTMAS MARKETS – BRUSSELS, BRUGES, LIÈGE

Festive lights, wooden stalls, and holiday decorations offer endless photo opportunities. Capture **glowing Ferris wheels, food stalls, and crowds** with long exposures or night mode settings.

## QUICK PHOTOGRAPHY CHECKLIST FOR BELGIUM

- Fully charged camera/phone
- Extra memory card or storage
- Power bank
- Travel tripod (for low light or night shots)

- Cleaning cloth (rain or fog happens!)
- Photo app or editing software for quick adjustments
- Respect for privacy—ask before photographing people

## CAPTURE THE ESSENCE OF BELGIUM

Photography in Belgium is more than just taking snapshots—it's about capturing the **mood, the detail, and the quiet beauty** that makes each place special. From city rooftops to forest trails, every corner of the country offers the chance to take home not just memories, but **timeless images** that tell your travel story.

CHAPTER

# 19 BELGIUM ITINERARIES – EXPLORE AT YOUR OWN PACE

> Whether you have just a couple of days or a full week, Belgium offers flexible travel options that blend world-famous landmarks with charming towns, scenic countryside, and rich local culture. The country's compact size and excellent public transport make it easy to see a lot—even on a short schedule.

In this chapter, you'll find **three ready-to-follow itineraries**:

- ✦ A quick **2-day sampler**,
- ✦ A well-rounded **5-day cultural getaway**, and
- ✦ A deep **7-day Belgium highlights tour**.

Each one is easy to customize to suit your pace, interests, and preferred travel style.

Antwerp[110]

# 2-DAY ITINERARY: CLASSIC BELGIUM SAMPLER

The cheeky Manneken Pis statue that often gets dresses up during the year[111]

**Perfect for:** First-time visitors with limited time

## DAY 1 – BRUSSELS

- Morning: Explore Grand Place and nearby Galeries Royales Saint-Hubert
- Midday: Visit the Atomium and nearby Mini-Europe
- Afternoon: See Manneken Pis, then head to the Mont des Arts for panoramic city views
- Evening: Dine in the Sablon district or near Place Sainte-Catherine

## DAY 2 – DAY TRIP TO BRUGES

- Morning: Take an early train to Bruges (~1 hour)
- Explore **Markt Square, the Belfry**, and **Burg Square**
- Afternoon: Enjoy a **canal boat tour**, visit the **Church of Our Lady**, and stroll along **Rozenhoedkaai**
- Evening: Return to Brussels or stay overnight in Bruges for a magical night walk

# 5-DAY ITINERARY: CULTURE, HISTORY & FOOD

**Perfect for:** Travelers seeking a mix of cities, museums, and culinary experiences

Treat yourself – enjoy mouth-watering local waffles[112]

### DAY 1 – BRUSSELS

- Focus on **museums**: Magritte Museum, BELvue, or Royal Museums of Fine Arts
- Try a local brewery or sample Belgian **moules-frites and beer pairings** in the evening

### DAY 2 – GHENT

- Travel to Ghent (30-40 minutes by train)
- Visit **Saint Bavo's Cathedral** and the **Ghent Altarpiece**
- Tour **Gravensteen Castle** and enjoy riverside cafés along **Graslei and Korenlei**
- Stay overnight or return to Brussels

### DAY 3 – BRUGES

- Explore the Groeningemuseum and Beguinage
- Sample local chocolates and waffles
- End the day with a sunset canal walk

### DAY 4 – LEUVEN OR MECHELEN

- Choose one of these small cities for a **relaxed day trip**
- **Leuven**: Town Hall, university vibe, and Stella Artois brewery
- **Mechelen**: Saint Rumbold's Cathedral, peaceful canals, and charming squares
- Return to Brussels in the evening

### DAY 5 – BRUSSELS MARKETS & FINAL TREATS

- Visit **local markets** (like Place du Jeu de Balle or Flagey)
- Shop for **souvenirs**, **chocolates**, or **Belgian beer gift packs**
- Enjoy a final **dinner in the city center**

# 7-DAY ITINERARY: BELGIUM HIGHLIGHTS TOUR

**Perfect for:** Travelers wanting to experience **a full range of Belgium's cities, nature, and culture**

The saxophone museum[113]

## DAY 1 – BRUSSELS

- Grand Place, Manneken Pis, and Atomium
- Evening in the historic center

## DAY 2 – ANTWERP

- Explore Cathedral of Our Lady, Grote Markt, and the MAS Museum
- Stroll through Zuid district or visit the fashion boutiques
- Return to Brussels or stay overnight

## DAY 3 – GHENT

- Morning train to Ghent
- Visit **Saint Bavo's Cathedral**, the Belfry, and Gravensteen
- Explore **Patershol district** and local beer cafés

## DAY 4 – BRUGES

- Full day in Bruges: canal tour, lace shops, and photo stops
- Optional: spend the night for a more peaceful evening atmosphere

## DAY 5 – DURBUY OR BOUILLON (ARDENNES)

- Rent a car or join a guided tour to the Ardennes
- Walk through **Durbuy's cobbled streets** or tour the **Castle of Bouillon**
- Enjoy regional dishes like **rabbit with prunes or venison stew**

## DAY 6 – DINANT & THE MEUSE VALLEY

- Take a Meuse River cruise
- Visit the Citadel of Dinant and the Saxophone Museum
- Return to Brussels or spend the night in Namur or Dinant

## DAY 7 – RELAX AND REFLECT IN BRUSSELS

- Light walking day: visit **Parc du Cinquantenaire**, have coffee in **Ixelles**, or shop in **Sablon**
- Wrap up your trip with a **chocolate tasting** or **Michelin-star meal**

## TIPS FOR PLANNING YOUR BELGIUM ITINERARY

✦ **Trains are fast and frequent** between major cities—use them to save time

✦ Base yourself in **Brussels, Ghent, or Antwerp** and do **day trips**

**A person relaxes while enjoying water views in Ghent**[14]

- Always check **museum opening hours** (many are closed Mondays)
- Don't overpack your schedule—Belgium is best enjoyed slowly
- For countryside stops, renting a car is helpful but not essential

## BUILD YOUR OWN BELGIAN EXPERIENCE

Every traveler is different—and Belgium is ready to match your pace. Whether you want to hop between cities, hike through green valleys, or sit for hours sipping Trappist beer by a quiet canal, these itineraries are here to guide and inspire.

# APPENDIX: WHERE TO FIND KEY LANDMARKS IN THIS GUIDE

> This appendix is your quick-reference tool for locating Belgium's key landmarks, museums, photo spots, and experiences mentioned throughout the guide. It's organized by city or region, along with references to the relevant chapters. Use it for planning routes, building custom itineraries, or finding nearby highlights.

## BRUSSELS

- ✓ **Grand Place** – *Chapters 2, 16, 17*
- ✓ **Manneken Pis** – *Chapters 2, 16*
- ✓ **Atomium** – *Chapters 2, 16, 17*
- ✓ **Mont des Arts** – *Chapters 2, 17*
- ✓ **Galeries Royales Saint-Hubert** – *Chapters 2, 15*
- ✓ **Magritte Museum** – *Chapters 4, 18*
- ✓ **Royal Museums of Fine Arts** – *Chapters 4, 18*
- ✓ **BELvue Museum** – *Chapter 4*
- ✓ **Parc du Cinquantenaire** – *Chapter 4, 18*
- ✓ **Sablon District (antiques, dining)** – *Chapters 4, 15, 18*
- ✓ **Delirium Café** – *Chapters 9, 16*
- ✓ **Mini-Europe** – *Chapter 18*
- ✓ **Christmas Market (Winter Wonders)** – *Chapter 14*

## BRUGES

- ✓ **Rozenhoedkaai** – *Chapters 5, 16, 17*
- ✓ **Markt Square** – *Chapter 5*
- ✓ **Belfry of Bruges** – *Chapters 5, 16, 17*
- ✓ **Basilica of the Holy Blood** – *Chapter 5*
- ✓ **Church of Our Lady (Michelangelo's Madonna)** – *Chapter 5*
- ✓ **Beguinage (Begijnhof)** – *Chapter 5*
- ✓ **Groeningemuseum** – *Chapters 5, 18*
- ✓ **Choco-Story Museum** – *Chapters 5, 15*
- ✓ **Canal Boat Tour** – *Chapters 5, 16, 17*
- ✓ **Bruges Christmas Market** – *Chapter 14*
- ✓ **Steenstraat / Katelijnestraat (Shopping)** – *Chapter 15*

## GHENT

- ✓ **Saint Bavo's Cathedral & Ghent Altarpiece** – *Chapters 6, 16, 17*
- ✓ **Gravensteen Castle** – *Chapters 6, 18*
- ✓ **Belfry of Ghent** – *Chapters 6, 16, 17*
- ✓ **St. Michael's Bridge** – *Chapters 6, 17*
- ✓ **Patershol District** – *Chapters 6, 15*
- ✓ **STAM – Ghent City Museum** – *Chapter 6*
- ✓ **S.M.A.K. – Contemporary Art Museum** – *Chapter 6*
- ✓ **MSK – Museum of Fine Arts** – *Chapter 6*
- ✓ **Vrijdagmarkt (Friday Market)** – *Chapter 6, 15*
- ✓ **Gentse Feesten (City Festival)** – *Chapter 14*
- ✓ **Light Plan (Night Lighting Walk)** – *Chapters 6, 16*

## ANTWERP

- ✓ **Cathedral of Our Lady** – *Chapters 7, 16*
- ✓ **Grote Markt** – *Chapter 7*
- ✓ **MAS (Museum aan de Stroom)** – *Chapters 7, 18*
- ✓ **Red Star Line Museum** – *Chapter 7*
- ✓ **Rubenshuis (Rubens House)** – *Chapter 7*
- ✓ **Antwerp Central Station** – *Chapters 7, 16, 17*
- ✓ **De Koninck Brewery** – *Chapters 7, 9*
- ✓ **Meir / Nationalestraat (Shopping Districts)** – *Chapter 15*
- ✓ **Stadsfeestzaal Shopping Hall** – *Chapter 15*

## LEUVEN

- ✓ **Oude Markt (Longest Bar in the World)** – *Chapters 8, 16*
- ✓ **Leuven Town Hall** – *Chapters 8, 16, 17*
- ✓ **Stella Artois Brewery** – *Chapter 8*
- ✓ **Botanic Garden** – *Chapter 8*
- ✓ **Comics / Fashion Shops** – *Chapter 15*
- ✓ **Leuven Christmas Market** – *Chapter 14*

## MECHELEN

- ✓ **St. Rumbold's Cathedral & Tower** – *Chapters 8, 18*
- ✓ **Groot Begijnhof** – *Chapter 8*
- ✓ **Technopolis (Science for Kids)** – *Chapter 8*
- ✓ **Canals & Old Town** – *Chapter 8*
- ✓ **Shopping Streets & Souvenirs** – *Chapter 15*

## DINANT & THE MEUSE VALLEY

- ✓ **Collegiate Church of Our Lady** - *Chapters 3, 16*
- ✓ **Citadel of Dinant** - *Chapters 8, 18*
- ✓ **Meuse River Cruise** - *Chapters 8, 16, 18*
- ✓ **Caves of Dinant (La Merveilleuse)** - *Chapter 3*

## WALLONIA & ARDENNES

- ✓ **Durbuy (Old Town)** - *Chapters 8, 16*
- ✓ **Bouillon / Château de Bouillon** - *Chapters 8, 16, 18*
- ✓ **Orval Abbey** - *Chapter 10*
- ✓ **Han-sur-Lesse & Caves of Han** - *Chapters 3, 10, 17*
- ✓ **Spa (Town, Thermal Baths)** - *Chapters 10, 18*
- ✓ **High Fens (Hautes Fagnes)** - *Chapters 3, 10*
- ✓ **Binche Carnival** - *Chapter 14*
- ✓ **Ducasse d'Ath (Giants Parade)** - *Chapter 14*
- ✓ **Fête de la Wallonie (Namur)** - *Chapter 14*
- ✓ **Grand-Hornu (UNESCO Industrial Site)** - *Chapter 17*

## COASTAL BELGIUM

- ✓ **Zwin Nature Park – Knokke-Heist** - *Chapters 3, 17*
- ✓ **Nieuwpoort & Oostduinkerke (Beach Adventures)** - *Chapter 10*
- ✓ **De Panne (Sand Yachting)** - *Chapter 10*
- ✓ **De Haan, Ostend** - *Chapter 3*
- ✓ **Belgian Coast Tram (Kusttram)** - *Chapter 3*

## SHOPPING, MARKETS & SOUVENIRS

- ✓ **Galeries Royales Saint-Hubert – Brussels** – *Chapters 2, 15*
- ✓ **Place du Jeu de Balle Market – Brussels** – *Chapter 15*
- ✓ **Flagey Market – Brussels** – *Chapter 15*
- ✓ **Vrijdagmarkt – Ghent** – *Chapter 15*
- ✓ **Antwerp Exotic Market (Saturdays)** – *Chapter 15*
- ✓ **Choco-Story / Chocolate Boutiques** – *Chapters 5, 9, 15*
- ✓ **Comic Book Shops (Tintin, Smurfs)** – *Chapter 15*
- ✓ **Lace Stores – Bruges** – *Chapter 15*
- ✓ **Speculoos, Cuberdons, Pralines (Food Gifts)** – *Chapters 9, 15*

## SEASONAL HIGHLIGHTS & EVENTS

- ✓ **Floralia Spring Flower Show – Brussels** – *Chapter 14*
- ✓ **Hallerbos Bluebell Forest – Halle** – *Chapters 3, 14, 16, 17*
- ✓ **Open Monument Day – Nationwide** – *Chapter 14*
- ✓ **Zythos Beer Festival – Leuven** – *Chapter 14*
- ✓ **Brussels Design September** – *Chapter 14*
- ✓ **Christmas Markets – Brussels, Bruges, Ghent, Liège** – *Chapter 14*
- ✓ **Tomorrowland Festival – Boom** – *Chapter 14*
- ✓ **Carnival of Binche – Wallonia** – *Chapter 14*

## CURRENCY & MONEY REFERENCE

- ✓ **Currency (Euro), ATMs, Credit Cards** – *Chapter 14*
- ✓ **Tipping Etiquette** – *Chapter 14*
- ✓ **VAT Refund for Non-EU Visitors** – *Chapter 14*
- ✓ **Exchange Advice & Using Cash** – *Chapter 14*

## NEED MORE INFO? JUMP BACK TO...

- ✓ **Getting Around Belgium** → *Chapter 1*
- ✓ **Top Landmarks by City** → *Chapters 2-7*
- ✓ **Hidden Gems & Small Towns** → *Chapter 8*
- ✓ **Food & Drink Culture** → *Chapter 9*
- ✓ **Outdoor Adventures** → *Chapter 10*
- ✓ **Day Trips** → *Chapter 11*
- ✓ **Where to Stay** → *Chapter 12*
- ✓ **Culture, Etiquette & Phrases** → *Chapter 13*
- ✓ **Currency & Money Matters** → *Chapter 14*
- ✓ **Events & Festivals** → *Chapter 15*
- ✓ **Shopping & Souvenirs** → *Chapter 16*
- ✓ **Top Photo Spots** → *Chapter 17*
- ✓ **Ready-Made Itineraries** → *Chapter 18*

## FINAL TRAVEL TIP

Save this appendix to quickly **locate places during your trip**, build your itinerary on the go, or find new ideas while exploring. Belgium is full of unforgettable moments—this guide helps you find them faster, and experience them better.

## Here's another book by Captivating Travels that you might like

# Welcome Aboard, Discover
## Your Limited-Time Free Bonus!

Hello, traveler! Welcome to the Captivating Travels family, and thanks for grabbing a copy of this book! Since you've chosen to join us on this journey, we'd like to offer you something special.

Check out the link below for a FREE Ultimate Travel Checklist eBook & Printable PDF to make your travel planning stress-free and enjoyable.

But that's not all - you'll also gain access to our exclusive email list with even more free e-books and insider travel tips. Well, what are you waiting for? Click the link below to join and embark on your next adventure with ease.

Access your bonus here: **https://livetolearn.lpages.co/checklist/**
**Or, Scan the QR code!**

# IMAGE SOURCES

1. Fred Romero from Paris, France, CC BY 2.0 <https://creativecommons.org/licenses/by/2.0>, via Wikimedia Commons https://commons.wikimedia.org/w/index.php?curid=78794359

2. dennis and aimee jonez, CC BY-SA 2.0 <https://creativecommons.org/licenses/by-sa/2.0>, via Wikimedia Commons https://commons.wikimedia.org/w/index.php?curid=2795352

3. Jean Housen, CC BY-SA 4.0 <https://creativecommons.org/licenses/by-sa/4.0>, via Wikimedia Commons https://commons.wikimedia.org/w/index.php?curid=68091936

4. www.openstreetmap.org

5. www.openstreetmap.org

6. www.openstreetmap.org

7. www.openstreetmap.org

8. Trougnouf (Benoit Brummer), CC BY 4.0 <https://creativecommons.org/licenses/by/4.0>, via Wikimedia Commons https://commons.wikimedia.org/w/index.php?curid=77527737

9. Vitaly Volkov/Волков Виталий Сергеевич, CC BY 2.5 <https://creativecommons.org/licenses/by/2.5>, via Wikimedia Commons https://commons.wikimedia.org/w/index.php?curid=851260

10. Image by Dimitris Vetsikas from Pixabay https://pixabay.com/photos/brugge-markt-square-buildings-3626776/

11. www.openstreetmap.org

12. Marek Śliwecki, CC BY-SA 4.0 <https://creativecommons.org/licenses/by-sa/4.0>, via Wikimedia Commons https://commons.wikimedia.org/w/index.php?curid=117430735

13. www.openstreetmap.org

14. www.openstreetmap.org

15   www.openstreetmap.org

16   Rolf Kranz, CC BY-SA 4.0 <https://creativecommons.org/licenses/by-sa/4.0>, via Wikimedia Commons https://commons.wikimedia.org/w/index.php?curid=76441421

17   www.openstreetmap.org

18   www.openstreetmap.org

19   Jim Linwood, CC BY 2.0 <https://creativecommons.org/licenses/by/2.0>, via Wikimedia Commons https://commons.wikimedia.org/w/index.php?curid=6818817

20   www.openstreetmap.org

21   Jean-Pol GRANDMONT, CC BY 3.0 <https://creativecommons.org/licenses/by/3.0>, via Wikimedia Commons https://commons.wikimedia.org/w/index.php?curid=9942412

22   David Edgar, CC BY-SA 3.0 <https://creativecommons.org/licenses/by-sa/3.0>, via Wikimedia Commons https://commons.wikimedia.org/w/index.php?curid=4477742

23   By Thomas Faunce - Own work, CC0, https://commons.wikimedia.org/w/index.php?curid=8661252

24   By Gary Houston - Own work, CC0, https://commons.wikimedia.org/w/index.php?curid=27865871

25   www.openstreetmap.org

26   © Anil Öztas, CC BY-SA 4.0 <https://creativecommons.org/licenses/by-sa/4.0>, via Wikimedia Commons https://commons.wikimedia.org/w/index.php?curid=134568534

27   Image by Jochen Schaft from Pixabay https://pixabay.com/photos/belgium-brussels-tourism-3605546/

28   Photo by Paul Deetman from Pexels: https://www.pexels.com/photo/photo-of-parc-du-cinquantenaire-2960887/

29   Photo by lil artsy: https://www.pexels.com/photo/worms-eye-view-of-the-atomium-1595086/

30  Photo by Magda Ehlers: https://www.pexels.com/photo/facade-of-the-mont-des-arts-building-in-brussels-belgium-12798572/

31  Voyager747, CC BY-SA 4.0 <https://creativecommons.org/licenses/by-sa/4.0>, via Wikimedia Commons https://commons.wikimedia.org/w/index.php?curid=50410130

32  By Romaine - Own work, CC0, https://commons.wikimedia.org/w/index.php?curid=77800216

33  Photo by Elifinatlasi : https://www.pexels.com/photo/woman-holding-a-cardboard-tray-with-waffle-decorated-with-chocolate-and-strawberries-18165128/

34  KoS, CC BY-SA 3.0 <https://creativecommons.org/licenses/by-sa/3.0>, via Wikimedia Commons https://commons.wikimedia.org/w/index.php?curid=10798384

35  Michel wal, CC BY-SA 3.0 <https://creativecommons.org/licenses/by-sa/3.0>, via Wikimedia Commons https://commons.wikimedia.org/w/index.php?curid=15836094

36  Autoworld, CC BY-SA 4.0 <https://creativecommons.org/licenses/by-sa/4.0>, via Wikimedia Commons https://commons.wikimedia.org/w/index.php?curid=44349101

37  Filharmoniker, CC BY-SA 4.0 <https://creativecommons.org/licenses/by-sa/4.0>, via Wikimedia Commons https://commons.wikimedia.org/w/index.php?curid=53032298

38  Photo by CEphoto, Uwe Aranas https://commons.wikimedia.org/w/index.php?curid=34567077

39  storem (Tim Dobbelaere) profile, CC BY-SA 2.0 <https://creativecommons.org/licenses/by-sa/2.0>, via Wikimedia Commons, https://commons.wikimedia.org/w/index.php?curid=9475899

40  Wolfgang Staudt [1], CC BY 2.0 <https://creativecommons.org/licenses/by/2.0>, via Wikimedia Commons https://commons.wikimedia.org/w/index.php?curid=16155598

41  Superchilum, CC BY-SA 3.0 <https://creativecommons.org/licenses/by-sa/3.0>, via Wikimedia Commons https://commons.wikimedia.org/w/index.php?curid=22570608

42  *Elke Wetzig (elya), CC BY-SA 2.0 DE <https://creativecommons.org/licenses/by-sa/2.0/de/deed.en>, via Wikimedia Commons https://commons.wikimedia.org/w/index.php?curid=55779*

43  *Wolfgang Staudt, CC BY 2.0 <https://creativecommons.org/licenses/by/2.0>, via Wikimedia Commons https://commons.wikimedia.org/w/index.php?curid=4278526*

44  *Navy8300, CC BY-SA 3.0 <https://creativecommons.org/licenses/by-sa/3.0>, via Wikimedia Commons https://commons.wikimedia.org/w/index.php?curid=21788175*

45  *Tania Dey, CC BY-SA 3.0 <https://creativecommons.org/licenses/by-sa/3.0>, via Wikimedia Commons https://commons.wikimedia.org/w/index.php?curid=28598508*

46  *Spotter2, CC BY-SA 3.0 <https://creativecommons.org/licenses/by-sa/3.0>, via Wikimedia Commons https://commons.wikimedia.org/w/index.php?curid=4407752*

47  *www.openstreetmap.org*

48  *www.openstreetmap.org*

49  *Photo by Dylan Chan: https://www.pexels.com/photo/iconic-medieval-architecture-along-the-waterside-in-ghent-30427221/*

50  *Photo by Gonzalo Facello: https://www.pexels.com/photo/ground-level-shot-of-the-saint-nicholas-church-in-ghent-14983034/*

51  *Photo by Anuja Dangol: https://www.pexels.com/photo/view-of-the-gravensteen-castle-ghent-east-flanders-in-belgium-2538363/*

52  *https://commons.wikimedia.org/w/index.php?curid=150003374*

53  *www.openstreetmap.org*

54  *Thomas Kindermans, CC BY-SA 3.0 <https://creativecommons.org/licenses/by-sa/3.0>, via Wikimedia Commons https://commons.wikimedia.org/w/index.php?curid=11111136*

55  *www.Openstreetmap.org*

56  Paul Hermans, CC BY-SA 3.0 <https://creativecommons.org/licenses/by-sa/3.0>, via Wikimedia Commons https://commons.wikimedia.org/w/index.php?curid=11780039

57  https://commons.wikimedia.org/w/index.php?curid=8982313

58  https://commons.wikimedia.org/w/index.php?curid=11954700

59  Image by Donna Sarjeant from Pixabay https://pixabay.com/photos/werregarenstraat-graffiti-alley-4700462/

60  Image by peter verhelst from Pixabay https://pixabay.com/photos/ghent-jacob-van-artevelde-2592514/

61  Photo by Max Avans: https://www.pexels.com/photo/photo-of-building-facade-5067323/

62  Photo by Wolfgang Weiser from Pexels: https://www.pexels.com/photo/central-station-platform-with-historic-architecture-29428867/

63  Alvesgaspar, CC BY-SA 4.0 <https://creativecommons.org/licenses/by-sa/4.0>, via Wikimedia Commons https://commons.wikimedia.org/w/index.php?curid=44472913

64  DRG-fan, CC BY-SA 4.0 <https://creativecommons.org/licenses/by-sa/4.0>, via Wikimedia Commons https://commons.wikimedia.org/w/index.php?curid=62039652

65  Photo by Antonia Maria Thomassen : https://www.pexels.com/photo/majestic-interior-of-historic-train-station-30006269/

66  Zinneke, CC BY-SA 3.0 <https://creativecommons.org/licenses/by-sa/3.0>, via Wikimedia Commons https://commons.wikimedia.org/w/index.php?curid=50173630

67  Velvet, CC BY-SA 3.0 <https://creativecommons.org/licenses/by-sa/3.0>, via Wikimedia Commons https://commons.wikimedia.org/w/index.php?curid=4727625

68  Kristina D.C. Hoeppner, CC BY-SA 2.0 <https://creativecommons.org/licenses/by-sa/2.0>, via Wikimedia Commons https://commons.wikimedia.org/w/index.php?curid=18325853

**69** Roger Price from Antwerp, Belgium, CC BY 2.0 <https://creativecommons.org/licenses/by/2.0>, via Wikimedia Commons https://commons.wikimedia.org/w/index.php?curid=1242970

**70** https://www.flickr.com/photos/jiuguangw/, CC BY-SA 2.0 <https://creativecommons.org/licenses/by-sa/2.0>, via Wikimedia Commons https://commons.wikimedia.org/w/index.php?curid=30455346

**71** Photo by Boris Ivas: https://www.pexels.com/photo/city-bridge-with-saxophone-festival-installation-6848857/

**72** Donar Reiskoffer, CC BY 3.0 <https://creativecommons.org/licenses/by/3.0>, via Wikimedia Commons https://commons.wikimedia.org/w/index.php?curid=13282129

**73** Juan V. Vera del Campo from Tarragona, Spain, CC BY-SA 2.0 <https://creativecommons.org/licenses/by-sa/2.0>, via Wikimedia Commons https://commons.wikimedia.org/w/index.php?curid=77976521

**74** Steven Fruitsmaak, CC BY-SA 3.0 <http://creativecommons.org/licenses/by-sa/3.0/>, via Wikimedia Commons https://commons.wikimedia.org/w/index.php?curid=1771692

**75** Trougnouf (Benoit Brummer), CC BY 4.0 <https://creativecommons.org/licenses/by/4.0>, via Wikimedia Commons https://commons.wikimedia.org/w/index.php?curid=74423118

**76** Image by Loyloy Thal from Pixabay https://pixabay.com/photos/bouillon-ardennes-belgium-jlow-2412823/

**77** Image by Dylan Leagh from Pixabay https://pixabay.com/photos/bouillon-castle-town-belgium-river-7052397/

**78** Donar Reiskoffer, CC BY-SA 3.0 <http://creativecommons.org/licenses/by-sa/3.0/>, via Wikimedia Commons https://commons.wikimedia.org/w/index.php?curid=14785

**79** Image by Siggy Nowak from Pixabay https://pixabay.com/photos/oudenaarde-sculpture-metallic-1098617/

**80** Jean-Pol GRANDMONT, CC BY-SA 3.0 <https://creativecommons.org/licenses/by-sa/3.0>, via Wikimedia Commons https://commons.wikimedia.org/w/index.php?curid=2698675

81  Jean-Pol GRANDMONT, CC BY-SA 3.0 <https://creativecommons.org/licenses/by-sa/3.0>, via Wikimedia Commons https://commons.wikimedia.org/w/index.php?curid=181221

82  Photo by Ricardo Oliveira: https://www.pexels.com/photo/retro-van-with-belgian-waffles-on-street-of-brussels-belgium-21833100/

83  User: (WT-shared) Jpatokal at wts wikivoyage, CC BY-SA 4.0 <https://creativecommons.org/licenses/by-sa/4.0>, via Wikimedia Commons https://commons.wikimedia.org/w/index.php?curid=22921370

84  ayustety from Tokyo, Japan, CC BY-SA 2.0 <https://creativecommons.org/licenses/by-sa/2.0>, via Wikimedia Commons https://commons.wikimedia.org/w/index.php?curid=3438247

85  Jon Åslund, CC BY 2.0 <https://creativecommons.org/licenses/by/2.0>, via Wikimedia Commons https://commons.wikimedia.org/w/index.php?curid=14971242

86  FlippyFlink, CC BY-SA 4.0 <https://creativecommons.org/licenses/by-sa/4.0>, via Wikimedia Commons https://commons.wikimedia.org/w/index.php?curid=114406461

87  Photo by Lies: https://www.pexels.com/photo/canal-in-city-15882823/

88  Photo by Laura Paredis: https://www.pexels.com/photo/people-on-historic-town-square-13095194/

89  Thundercloud at the English-language Wikipedia, CC BY-SA 3.0 <http://creativecommons.org/licenses/by-sa/3.0/>, via Wikimedia Commons https://commons.wikimedia.org/w/index.php?curid=6208012

90  www.openstreetmap.org

91  https://commons.wikimedia.org/w/index.php?curid=17984344

92  Jean-Pol GRANDMONT, CC BY 2.0 <https://creativecommons.org/licenses/by/2.0>, via Wikimedia Commons https://commons.wikimedia.org/w/index.php?curid=208521

93  Marlinde Dwarswaard, CC BY-SA 4.0 <https://creativecommons.org/licenses/by-sa/4.0>, via Wikimedia Commons https://commons.wikimedia.org/w/index.php?curid=152009047

94  Photo by Ad Thiry: https://www.pexels.com/photo/scenic-view-of-bruges-town-hall-in-belgium-30034918/

95  https://pixabay.com/photos/grand-place-brussels-belgium-europe-6577511/

96  https://pixabay.com/photos/bruges-market-square-city-markt-6574714/

97  Photo by Sebastian Luna: https://www.pexels.com/photo/historic-castle-like-building-in-ghent-belgium-28428169/

98  Photo by Laura Paredis: https://www.pexels.com/photo/interior-of-the-antwerpe-museum-in-belgium-25424643/

99  Image by Dimitris Vetsikas from Pixabay https://pixabay.com/photos/belgium-brussels-festival-puppet-3590800/

100  Photo by Johannes Eeckmann: https://www.pexels.com/photo/people-on-the-seaside-restaurant-4575823/

101  Christophe Degryse, CC BY-SA 4.0 <https://creativecommons.org/licenses/by-sa/4.0>, via Wikimedia Commons https://commons.wikimedia.org/w/index.php?curid=61595177

102  Image by Ji-Sun Yoo from Pixabay https://pixabay.com/photos/brussels-europe-belgium-bruxelles-1017978/

103  Image by Ji-Sun Yoo from Pixabay https://pixabay.com/photos/brussels-europe-belgium-bruxelles-1017977/

104  Gordito1869, CC BY 3.0 <https://creativecommons.org/licenses/by/3.0>, via Wikimedia Commons https://commons.wikimedia.org/w/index.php?curid=34396976

105  Photo by Vish Pix: https://www.pexels.com/photo/a-low-angle-shot-of-people-walking-on-the-street-near-the-building-14424758/

106  Photo by Logan Hamm: https://www.pexels.com/photo/chocolate-store-in-belgium-24596157/

107  Ank Kumar, CC BY-SA 4.0 <https://creativecommons.org/licenses/by-sa/4.0>, via Wikimedia Commons https://commons.wikimedia.org/w/index.php?curid=99450491

108  *Image by Ben Kerckx from Pixabay* https://pixabay.com/photos/nature-forest-hallerbos-hyacinth-5045307/

109  *Image by Dimitris Vetsikas from Pixabay* https://pixabay.com/photos/ghent-belgium-architecture-travel-3680330/

110  *Image by Andreas from Pixabay* https://pixabay.com/photos/antwerp-belgium-architecture-6614695/

111  *Trougnouf (Benoit Brummer), CC BY 4.0* <https://creativecommons.org/licenses/by/4.0>*, via Wikimedia Commons,* https://commons.wikimedia.org/w/index.php?curid=72876013

112  *Photo by Luca Nardone:* https://www.pexels.com/photo/person-holding-box-of-waffle-4377110/

113  *Ymnes, CC BY-SA 4.0* <https://creativecommons.org/licenses/by-sa/4.0>*, via Wikimedia Commons By Ymnes - Own work, CC BY-SA 4.0,* https://commons.wikimedia.org/w/index.php?curid=73253579

114  *Photo by Viktor Mogilat :* https://www.pexels.com/photo/person-sitting-on-pavement-beside-body-of-water-3979108/

Printed in Dunstable, United Kingdom